el Huber
N90/F90

Magic Lantern Guides
Proof of Purchase
NIKON
N90/F90

Michael Huber

Nikon F90

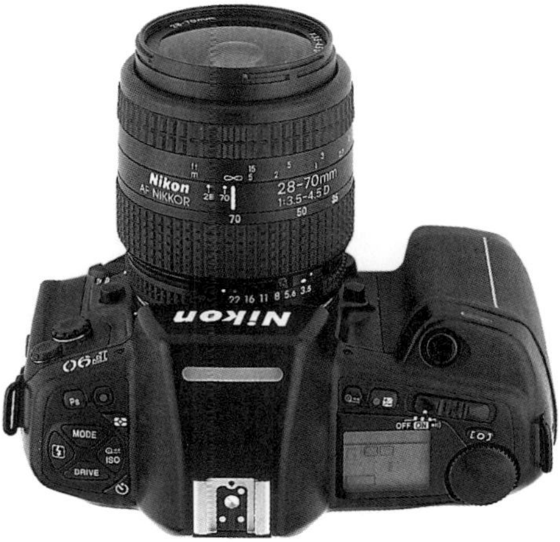

Laterna magica

Magic Lantern Guide to
Nikon N90/F90

A Laterna magica® book

First English Language Edition July, 1993
Published in the United States of America by

The Saunders Group
21 Jet View Drive
Rochester, NY 14624

From the original German edition by Michael Huber
Translated by Hayley Ohlig
Edited by Bob Shell
Editorial Assistant, David Hess
USA Production Coordinator, Marti Saltzman
With special thanks and appreciation to those behind the scenes who made the publication of this book possible.

Printed in Germany by Kösel GmbH, Kempten

ISBN 1-883403-01-4

Table of Contents

Introduction

Of the modern Nikon SLR's, the N2000/F-301, introduced in 1985, was the first Nikon with a built-in motor drive, and is still popular although no longer in production. The N2020/F-501, the first autofocus SLR, was replaced fairly quickly by the N4004/F-401, introduced in 1987, and the N8008/F-801 in 1988. While the N4004s/F-401s and N5005/F-401X are intended for the advanced amateur, the N8008s/F-801s is regarded as the "semi-pro" Nikon. The F4, introduced in 1988, was met with skepticism at first, but since then has become widely accepted as the professional standard. With the many-featured N6006/F-601, Nikon filled the gap between the N4004 and N8008. At Photokina '92, the N90 was introduced. It was the first of a new camera generation and rounded out the Nikon line-up between the N8008s and F4. This book is based on three months worth of practical use of the N90/F90. The author, as well as amateurs and an experienced professional were involved in the testing. Included in the book are sample pictures illustrating exposure, flash technique, autofocus, etc., which were actually shot with the N90/F90.

Acknowledgments

I would particularly like to thank Mrs. Shultz, Mr. Exner, and Mr. Nagel of Nikon, who supplied the information necessary to complete this book. It is important to note that sections of this book which deal with the Data Link were written before any definite information or test unit was available.

This book deals with the N90/F90, F90D and F90S models. The latter two models are nothing more than the standard body with the Data Back or Multi-function Back, respectively. These are not available in North America. All statements within this book refer to all models, and any discrepancies are explained. In any event, it seems that for the time being Nikon is selling the N90/F90 and the optional backs separately.

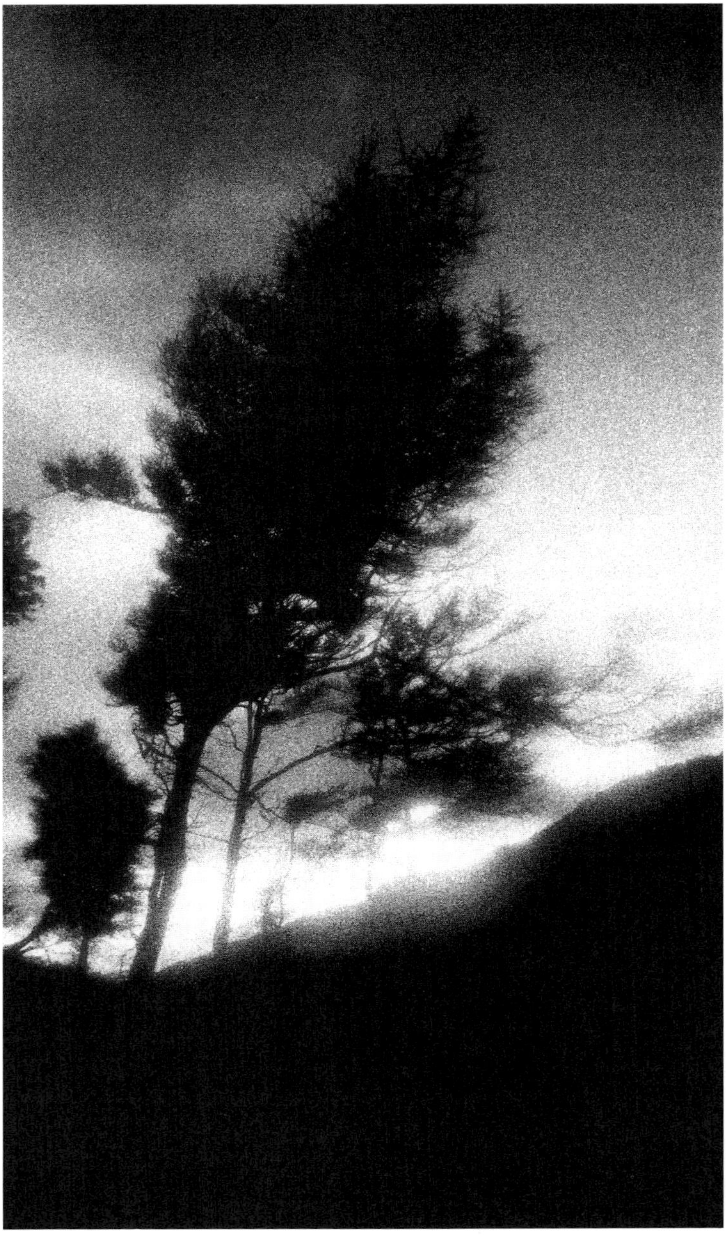

N90/F90 Technique

In this chapter you will find an overview of some of the N90/F90's most important features. And while the following subsections give you an introductory overview, many of the possibilities mentioned will be explained fully in subsequent chapters.

Unique Features

The N90/F90 retains and improves on important features of other Nikon cameras. Examining the Nikon cameras from a usability perspective, one has three alternatives with the fully automatic autofocus SLR's: The N6006 with a superfluity of knobs and functions, the F4 with its traditional settings and the N8008 with relatively clear, fully automatic functions. Regarding handling, the N8008 is, in my opinion, one of the best cameras available to date. It therefore seems doubtful that the new N90/F90 can be better in this respect. However, since the N90/F90 offers approximately 30% more functions than the N6006, N8008, and F4, it is unique in its operation.

Ergonomic Design

Those functions that are needed while the camera is at your eye can easily be reached on the N90/F90 (subject to the size of the user's hands and fingers, naturally). The only negative point I noticed is that the command dial of the N90/F90, although more easily reached than on the N8008, sticks out slightly less, which effectively negates this advantage. The price of better handling is that a whole series of functions (such as multiple exposure, bracketing, etc.) cannot be performed by the N90/F90 itself, necessitating the use of the MF-26 back. Compared to the N8008, the

This picturesque reproduction of a Scottish landscape was taken with a 20mm lens and a granily processed T-Max 3200. A special soft-focus filter was used during printing to create a slight haze effect.
Picture: Wolf Huber

N90/F90 is better in many respects: the new AF-mode switch, illuminated central LC display, more meaningful warning buzzers, and the (with Data Link) programmable shut-off time.

What is unfortunately missing on the N90/F90 (like the N8008 and F4) is the aperture readout in 1/2 or, even better, 1/3 stops (important when setting exposure in studio-type situations when using a flash or exposure meter), electronic aperture adjustment (still only done manually on the lens), continuous display of exposure compensation, and the ability to set the camera for repeat operation (useful in repro work, for example).

Professional Stability

The N90/F90 even more of a professional's camera than the N8008s. This is obvious in that it has a heavier and slightly larger body. In keeping with the practical need for robustness, Nikon did not go for smaller, lighter plastic in either the N90/F90 or the new AF-Nikkor Type D lenses. And while the experienced photographer will inevitably complain about the weight of the photo gear he or she has to lug around, he or she undoubtedly values the advantages of the massive cameras. Slightly larger and heavier cameras simply feel good to the touch.

Lens Compatability

The N90/F90 is compatible with the full range of the new AF-Nikkor Type D lenses and the resulting 3D exposure and flash automation. It can also take advantage of the lightning focusing speed of the modern AF-I Nikkors with their built-in motors, previously only possible with the F4. Naturally, all the previous AF-Nikkors are compatible in exposure mode "M," with manual focusing and center-weighted or spot metering. Non-AF Nikkors that are f/5.6 or faster can take advantage of the AF indicator in the viewfinder. Together with the AF teleconverter TC-16A, autofocus is possible using most non-AF fixed focal length lenses, provided the lens speed is faster than f/3.5.

Improved Autofocusing System

The autofocusing system on the N90/F90 is faster and more accurate than ever before.

❒ **"Dynamic focus" -** Nikon's name for predictive autofocus, it is always active on the N90/F90. That means that moving objects in the subject area are recognized and their position at the time of exposure is automatically calculated in all AF modes. The N6006, N8008s, and F4 already offered this feature, but only in selected modes.

❒ **Selectable area -** One of the main complaints professional Nikon users have had is the relatively small size of the focusing area on the N8008s and F4. I cannot completely subscribe to this, even though the argument that an autofocusing system works more reliably on a larger focusing area is valid. And for the snapshooter, it is a much more convenient tool. Regardless, the small field is definitely preferred after my tests on widely varied subjects. Those who do not concentrate as carefully when focusing, though, will no doubt have greater success with the larger AF area, which also has advantages regarding the 3D Matrix metering as well as 3D Matrix auto-flash. The crossfield-sensor captures complex structures with 246 horizontal and 74 vertical CCDs.

❒ **Faster -** The fact that the N90/F90's autofocusing system is somewhat faster than that of the N8008s or the F4 is due not only to the particularly fast AF motor, but also to the expanded mathematical capabilities of the camera's CPU (Central Processing Unit). Newly simplified and hence particularly fast formulae, commonly referred to as "Fuzzy Logic," were developed for the camera.

Advanced Metering Systems

Just like the N8008s and the F4, the N90/F90 offers Matrix, spot, and center-weighted metering options. When using Type D lenses, 3D Matrix metering is available.

❒ **Improved Matrix -** Unlike the N8008s and F4 which use five points in evaluating Matrix driven exposures, the N90/F90 uses eight. Unfortunately, however, these three additional points could not improve the result in certain critical cases, like pictures with lots of sky or very wispy subjects.

❒ **3D Matrix -** In this metering mode, the N90/F90 uses the autofocus to determine how to weight the various spots. In principal, this is a great idea, but the less-than-perfect pre-production N90/F90 used in our tests did not allow me to draw any qualitative conclusions.

Second Curtain Sync

The ability to synchronize the flash with the second (rear) shutter

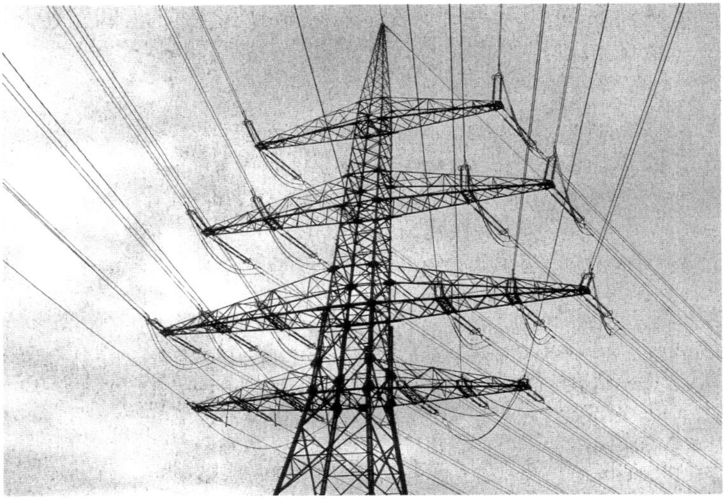

This high-voltage tower, photographed with appropriate perspective in silhouette, shows that even industrial structures can make interesting subjects.

curtain is very interesting. With normal sync, a moving object will "push" its motion blur ahead of itself, while with second curtain sync, it will "pull" its motion blur behind itself, the way it actually appears to the eye. With the N90/F90, this effect can be obtained using any one of the Nikon flashes.

Subject-specific Program Modes

The N90/F90 offers seven program modes that determine the optimal exposure/aperture combination based on the film speed, subject illumination, and lens speed. However, my tests showed that an experienced photographer, when given enough time to consider the subject, is often more accurate than the program modes on the N90/F90. This is definitely a function of the difference between human and computer "intelligence." The experienced pro knows what to do in borderline cases: For a sports

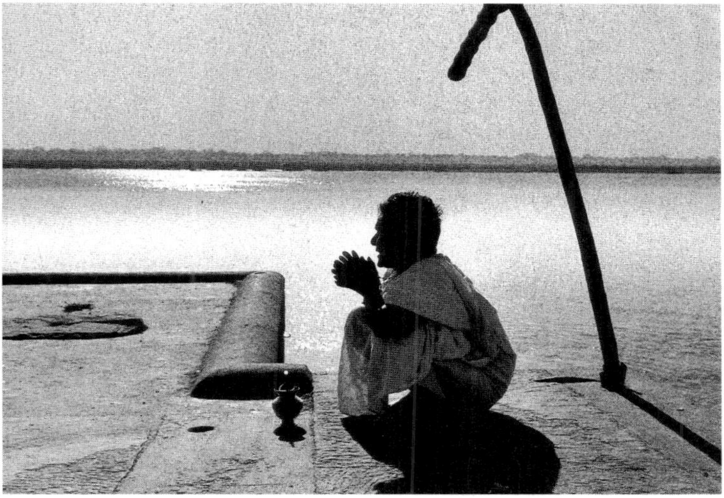

Far away from all tourist routes, this shot (Benares on the Ganges) mirrors the spirit and atmosphere of India.

shot with an exposure time between 1/250 and 1/500, do I take the faster or slower one? The computer has a 50/50 chance of being wrong. In the end, only the photographer knows what is more important: more blur or greater sharpness.

On the other hand, inexperienced photographers or pros working quickly inevitably make mistakes from time to time. In these situations, the program modes are practically infallible: even in extreme cases, it rarely deviates more than one stop or exposure interval from the optimal picture. Mind you, the photographer selects the program according to his or her natural limits. To do this, you need certain information which you will find in the appropriate chapters of this book.

Flash Photography

The shutter and the electronics of the N90/F90 make flash sync from 30 seconds to 1/4000 second possible, depending on the mode. Through this feature, the N90/F90 can use automatically controlled flashes to not only achieve optimal quality, but also to produce blurred effects and freeze motion. Using the exposure modes "P" and "A," the N90/F90's programmable "Slow" flash mode allows exposure times of up to 30 seconds, a great feature for ambient light or background intensity compensation.

Compatible Flash Units
Absolutely all of the N90/F90's flash functions can be utilized only with the SB-25. Practically all modern Nikon System Flashes can be used with the N90/F90, but depending on the model, certain functions will be unavailable.

N90/F90 Fundamentals

Camera type: Autofocus, 35mm single lens reflex with motorized film transport, electronic functions, and features optimized for professional use. Data Link connection for external remote display and remote control, programming, data storage, etc.

Film format: Film type 35mm; image size 24x36mm.

Lens mount: Nikon F-bayonet with additional electronic control and data transmission contacts for AF lenses with integrated motor connections. Additional electronic transmission of the absolute focus distance with Type D AF Nikkors and use of the internal motors of the AF-I Nikkors. Mechanical transmission of aperture with AI and AI-S Nikkors.

Autofocus system: Passive, with TTL phase detection and a cross-shaped autofocus sensor module. Size of measuring field is selectable. Working range: EV -1 to EV 19 at ISO 100 with 50mm f/1.4 lens. Dynamic autofocus in all AF modes. Particularly fast focus calculating algorithms.

Autofocus modes: 1) "S"= Single AF with sharpness priority: the shot will only be exposed when the image is in focus; when the shutter release is depressed halfway, the focus is stored.

2) "C"= Continuous autofocus with shutter priority: when the shutter release is depressed, the autofocus is constantly engaged (tracking autofocus) and an exposure can always be made, even if the autofocus has not completed focusing. "Dynamic autofocus," active in both "S" and "C" modes, constantly takes two measurements to identify moving objects and calculates the speed and direction of motion to predict the focus distance at the time of exposure.

Manual AF focus storage: Using the AF-L key; can also be combined with exposure storage using the MF-26 back. AF focusing assistance for manual focusing: The "electronic rangefinder" (autofocus confirmation indicator in the viewfinder) works with AF Nikkors and also with most AI and AI-S Nikkors that are f/5.6 or faster.

Metering modes: 1) Center-weighted metering (75/25 ratio). 2) Spot metering= In the center of the viewfinder, approximately 1% of the image area, range EV 3 to EV 21 (at ISO 100 and lens speed f/1.4). 3) Matrix metering= Eight zones metered, range EV 1 to EV 21 (at ISO 100 and lens speed f/1.4). Automatic exposure correction. 4) 3D Matrix metering= Special emphasis on the focused subject. Same range as above. Automatic correction.

Exposure automation: 1) Shutter priority ("S"). 2) Aperture priority ("A"). 3) Multi-program mode ("P"), with manual shift possible. 4) Manual ("M").

Subject optimized vari-programs: Seven options: 1) Portrait. 2) Portrait with flash and pre-flash. 3) Silhouette. 4) Large depth of field. 5) Landscape. 6) Sport. 7) Close-up.

Exposure value storage: Activated by pressing the AE-L knob; the last metered exposure value in all exposure modes is stored. Can be combined with focus storage using the MF-26 back or Data Link.

Manual exposure selection: Aperture on the lens, shutter speed on the central selector. The values are displayed in the viewfinder and on the external LCD. Relative brightness is displayed on a light scale using 1/3 stops. When setting relative to external exposure metering, i.e. when metering in a studio, the aperture must be set by feel, since the displays in the viewfinder and LCD show only full stops.

Exposure correction: Manually from -5 EV to +5 EV in increments of 1/3 EV (1 EV= 1 f-stop = 1 shutter speed interval). Automatic correction with Matrix metering or 3D Matrix metering.

Automatic bracketing: Only available with the Data Back MF-26 or Data Link. Three to 19 pictures with exposure differences from 1/3 to 2 EV.

Shutter: Electronically controlled, vertically travelling metal focal plane shutter made of a special light metal alloy. Electromagnetic release.

Shutter speeds: Stepless from 30 seconds to 1/8000 second and "bulb." Long exposures up to 99 hours 59 min. 59 sec. possible with the MF-26 Multi-function Back. The N90/F90 provides shutter release-controlled time exposures with the MC-20 remote control.

Shutter release: Electro-mechanical with 3 functions: 1) Touching it activates exposure metering for approximately 8 seconds. 2) Pressing it half way activates the autofocus and focus storage (in AF mode "S"). 3) Pressing it all the way activates the shutter. A separate camera power switch locks the shutter release. There is no mechanical cable release socket. Can be remotely triggered with the MC-20 cable. When using the MC-12A cable, the MC-25 adapter cable is necessary. Interval exposures possible using the MF-26.

Self-timer: Electronic. Delay is adjustable from 2 seconds to 30 seconds. Progress is shown by blinking LEDs on the camera body. Double self-timer in 10 second intervals is possible, as is cancellation before exposure.

3D Flash mode with test flash and multi-sensor metering. Regardless of whether or not the subject is centered or if the background is light or dark, flash pictures are correctly exposed with the N90/F90, the SB-25, and an AF-D lens.

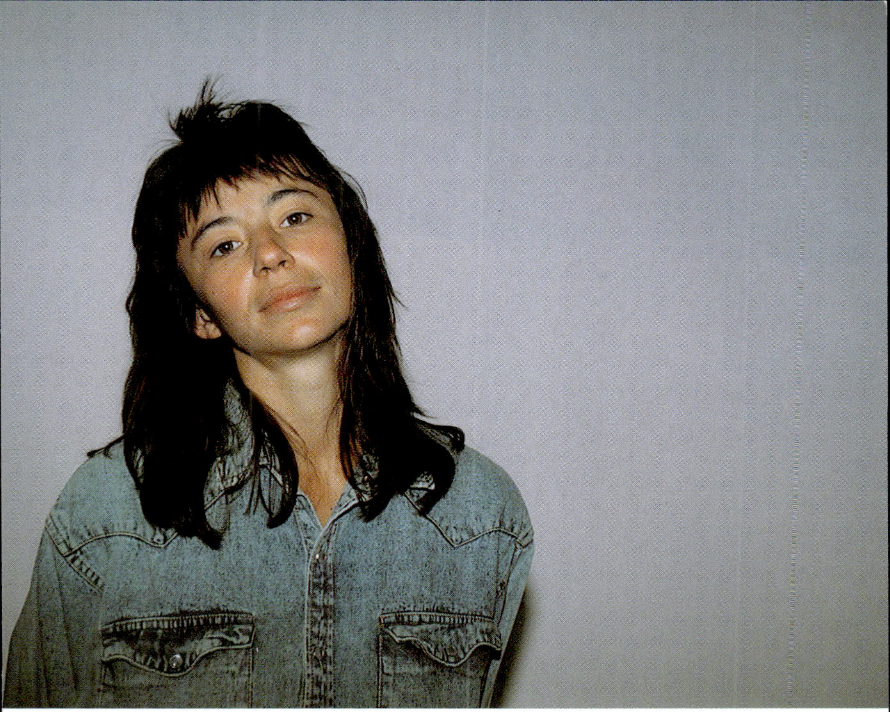

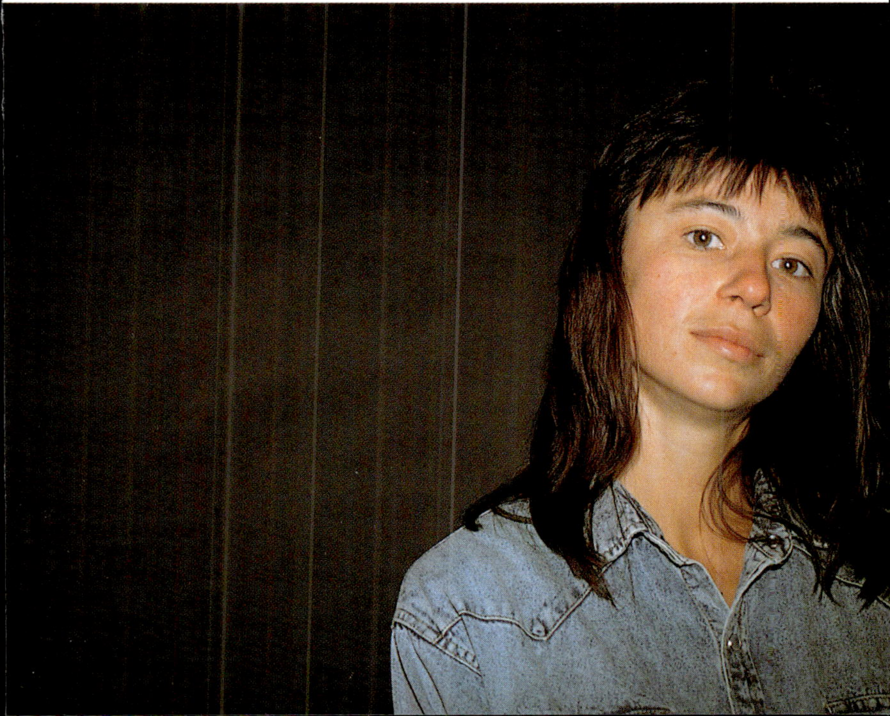

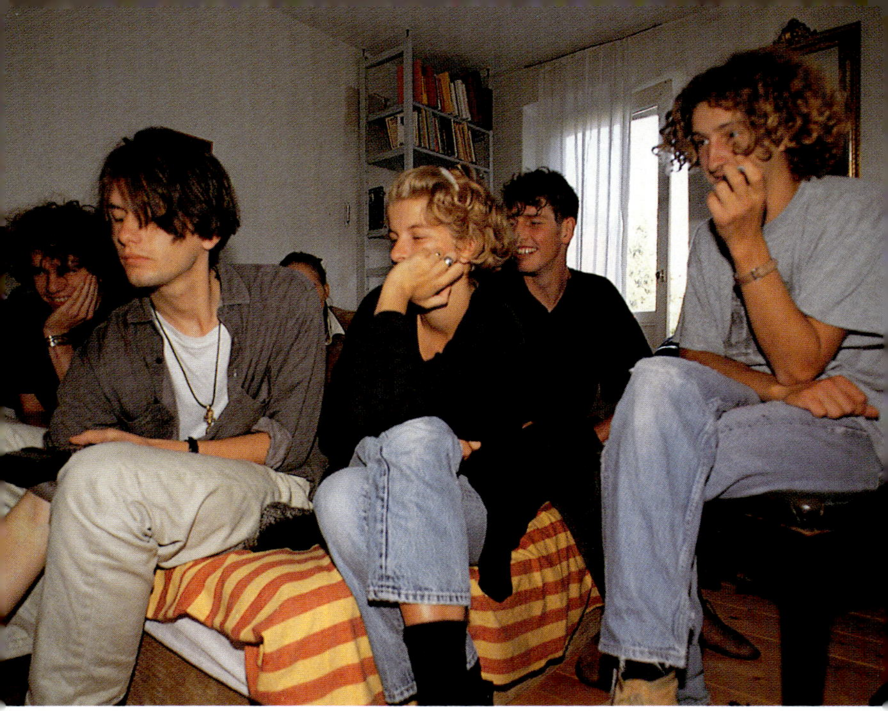

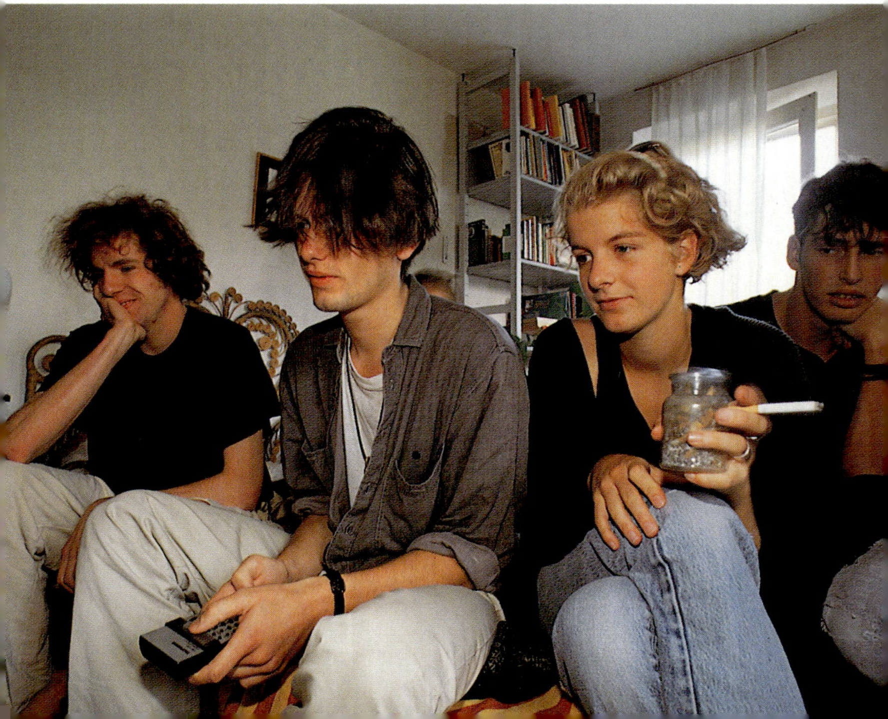

Multiple exposures: Only possible with the Data Back MF-26 or Data Link; 2 to 19 exposures possible on one image.

Viewfinder: Non-interchangeable, high eyepoint viewfinder with eye relief up to 19mm. Ninety-two percent of the image is shown at a magnification of of 0.78X (with a 50mm lens set at infinity). A built-in blind can be closed to prevent stray light from entering the viewfinder and causing incorrect metering when the eye is not close to the eyepiece.

Focusing screen: Supplied with Brite-View screen "type B," interchangeable with cross-hatch "type E."

Viewfinder displays: Continuous after touching the shutter release button. Displays AF focusing area size, focus indicator, exposure mode, shutter speed, aperture, frame counter, flash needed, and flash status when using a dedicated flash. When conditions warrant, viewfinder displays incorrect exposure warning, light scale or exposure correction advice, end of film, and exposure correction factor.

External LCD: 1) Constantly shown: Exposure mode, exposure metering mode, selected AF focusing area, frame counter, film transport, and transport error warnings. 2) Shown for approximately 8 seconds after touching the shutter release: Exposure time (including B), under- or over-exposure warning, aperture (full stops only), AF mode, manual focusing (if selected), flash mode (excluding normal TTL), film loaded, film transport verification, battery test, Data Link connected, and user programmed functions (via Data Link). 3) Shown after touching appropriate function key: film sensitivity, exposure correction factor, self-timer delay, and selected Vari-program.

While this background is unnaturally dark (f/5.6 at 1/60) when using normal sync and program mode (top), it is naturally brightened by switching to SLOW mode and using a shutter speed of 1/4 second (bottom). The motion blur overlaid on the flash exposure is just tolerable.

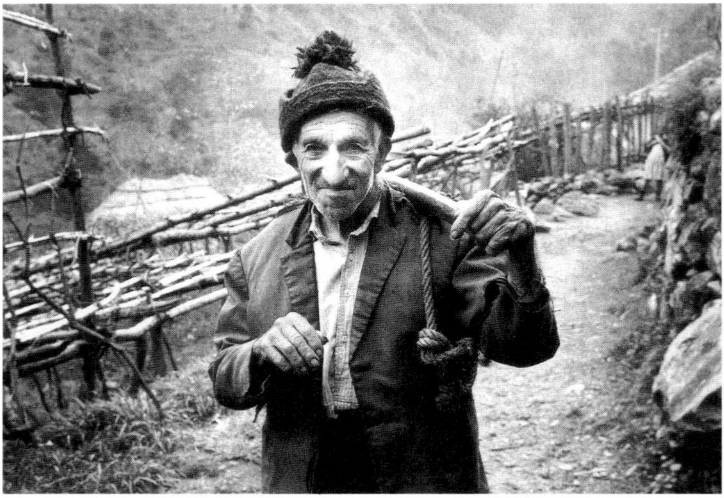

This portrait of a farm worker in the mountains of Madiera draws the surroundings into the image through the slightly fuzzy background.

Beeper: Can be turned off, and is intended as a warning, indicator, and system okay beeper. 1) Warnings: Aperture ring in "P" and "S" modes is not set to minimum, flash unit not set on TTL in "P" mode, under- and over-exposure, use of non-AF lenses with inappropriate mode, selecting bulb exposure time with inappropriate mode, camera shake (exposure times greater than 1/focal length in seconds) in "P" and "S" modes, film with erroneous or no DX code, and film transport problem. 2) Indicators: End of film, rewind complete, and self-timer progress. 3) Okay: Focusing in "S" mode complete.

Film sensitivity: Automatic DX from ISO 25 to ISO 5000 or manual from ISO 6 to ISO 6400.

Film loading: Automatically advances to first frame when shutter release is fully depressed. Correct loading and film advance is verified on LCD.

Film transport: Motor driven after each exposure, with three available modes: 1) Single exposure mode, "S." 2) Continuous exposure "L" (2 frames per second possible). 3) Continuous exposure "H" (3.6 frames per second possible). Successful film transport is verified on LCD. Auto-stop at the end of the film.

Counter: Additive counter, it counts backwards while film is being rewound.

Film rewind: By motor, it pulls the film leader into the cassette, but can be reprogrammed by Nikon Service to leave the leader out.

Depth of field preview: Press the depth-of-field preview button in "A" or "M" mode to visually verify the depth of field in the viewfinder.

Camera back: Can be replaced with one of two optional backs: 1) Data Back MF-25 (adds date and time to each frame). 2) Multifunction back MF-26 (see "Accessories for the N90/F90").

Flash mounting: Nikon dedicated flash shoe with ISO central contact as well as Nikon System contacts. ISO range for TTL flash is ISO 25 to ISO 1000. Use of flashes made by other manufacturers, especially older models, can damage the camera's electronics by overloading the circuits, and is therefore discouraged.

Flash sync control: 1) Normal: From 1/60 to 1/125 second in "P" and "A" modes. In "M" or "S" modes, the selected time will be used (times shorter than 1/250 will automatically be converted to 1/250). 2) Slow: In "P" and "A" modes, exposure times up to 30 seconds will be automatically set.

Second curtain sync: After selecting the flash function on the camera, all flashes will sync with the second curtain (with the SB-24 and SB-25 this setting is on the flash).

"FP" high-speed sync: With the SB-25, sync times from 1/250 second to 1/4000 second are possible.

Conventional TTL flash: Only possible with the SB-24 or SB-25, it is selected on the flash head itself.

Conventional TTL fill-flash: Automatically compensates for ambient light. The auto-flash sets the appropriate flash sync speed and/or aperture as well as adjusting the flash intensity based on an ambient light reading. During the exposure, the TTL flash duration is controlled using slightly center-weighted metering.

TTL fill-flash with Multi-Sensor: Same as above, but the TTL flash duration is controlled using a five-area Multi-Sensor reading.

Multi-Sensor fill-flash with monitor pre-flash: Only available when using the SB-25 and AF Nikkors, the flash fires a series of invisible test flashes that are analyzed by the Multi-Sensor. The auto-flash uses this information to gauge the spatial distribution of the subject as well as the reflective properties of the subject and background.

3D Multi-Sensor fill-flash with monitor pre-flash: Same as above, but available only when using Type D AF Nikkors, as focus distance is also used in the calculation. Together with the test flashes, non-central subjects and the extremely reflective objects in the frame are very accurately accounted for.

Manual flash exposure corrections: Can be set from +1 EV to +3 EV when using the SB-24 and SB-25. Correction is made on the flash unit itself. Also possible with other modern Nikon System flashes when using the Multi-function Back MF-26. (See "Special Accessories for the N90/F90").

This study in portraiture was taken somewhere on a Spanish street. ⇨

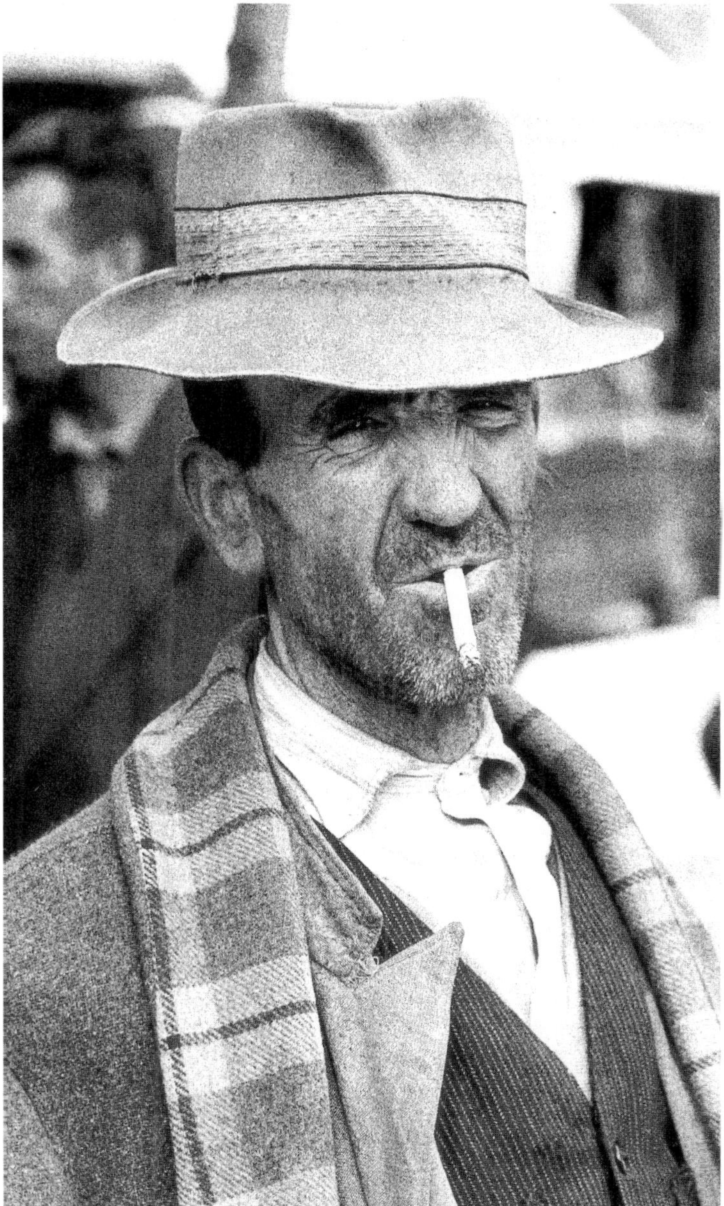

Flash bracketing: With Multi-control Back MF-26 or Data Link and all modern Nikon System flashes (see "Special Accessories for the N90/F90").

Flash confirmation display: A red LED lights in the viewfinder when the Nikon System flash is ready. It blinks or disappears if the flash was too weak to correctly illuminate the scene or if there was a bad contact between the flash and the hot-shoe.

Autofocus test flash: Possible when using an appropriate flash such as Nikon's SB-20, SB-22, SB-23, SB-24 and SB-25.

Camera power source: Four 1.5v alkaline AA-type batteries, good for up to 75 rolls (36 exposure) at 68°F(20°C), or 4 rechargeable NiCds of the same size, good for up to 55 rolls (36 exposure) at the same temperature.

Battery power confirmation: Aperture and shutter speed should be displayed for approximately 8 seconds when the shutter release is touched. Noticeably shorter display times are good indicators of low battery power. Additionally, a battery power display symbol is located on the LCD panel.

Size of camera body: Width: 6.5in. (154mm). Height: 4.5in. (106mm). Depth: 2.8in. (69mm) or 3in. (71mm) with Data Back. Weight: 27.7 ounces (775g), without batteries.

Special Accessories for the N90/F90

Eyepiece Adapter DK-7

To attach the waist-level viewer DR-3 or magnifying loupe DG-2.

Eye Cup DK-6

For more comfortable use, also serves to protect eyeglass lenses.

Viewfinder Screens

Viewfinder "type E" has a 12mm central circle, 2 AF focus brackets, and a vertical/horizontal grid on a fresnel lens. For reproduction work, architecture, and extreme wide-angle lenses.

External Battery Holder DB-6

With a six "AA" battery capacity, there is enough power to shoot approximately 10 times as many exposures. Ideal for continuous use in scientific documentation and high-speed sports photography.

Remote Release MC-20

For electrical remote triggering and long exposures ("T" shutter). The MC-12A in conjunction with the adapter cable MC-25 will accomplish the same thing (this combination is also necessary for autofocus preset focus in conjunction with the MF-26). Two N90/F90's can be simultaneously released using the MC-23 cable.

Data Back MF-25

Adds a choice of the following to the frame: 1) Year, month, and day. 2) Day, hour, and minute. 3) Day, month, and year. 4) World-time function. Also provides an alarm.

Multi-control Back MF-26

The following is only a brief list of the most important features. You will find practical instructions for using the MF-26 in the special chapter "Data and Multi-control Backs." Data that can be added to the frame includes: 1) Year, month, and day. 2) Day, hour, and minute. 3) Two-digit frame numbering. 4) Global numbering, either constant or increasing, from 1 to 999,999. 5) Shutter speed and aperture.

Other features include: 1) Continuous exposures, up to 19 per trigger release. 2) Interval timer (select time intervals between exposures from 1 second to 99 hours 59 min. 59 sec. Can also be combined with continuous mode. 3) Long exposures from 1 second to 99 hours 59 min. 59 sec. 4) Multiple exposures; 2 to 19 on one frame. 5) Automatic bracketing; 3 to 19 exposures with illumination differences from 1/3 to 2 EV. 6) Flash exposure correction; can be set from -3 EV to +1 EV in steps of 1/3. 7) Flash exposure bracketing; 3 to 19 exposures with illumination differences from 1/3 EV to 2 EV. 8) AE/AF storage provides simultaneous storage of exposure and distance settings. 9) AF sharpness priority in combination with manual distance selection and AF mode "C." 10) Preset autofocus automatically releases

shutter as soon as something moves into a pre-selected distance range. 11) Resets all camera functions (exposure metering, exposure mode, flash mode, and AF focusing area size) on demand. 12) Film transport can be freely programmed.
Some of the MF-26's functions can be reprogrammed using the Data Link.

Data Link System
The Data-Link (available in mid-1993) brings computer-controlled photography into the mainstream. Once connected to the Sharp "Wizard" (8000), the N90/F90 can be completely controlled by remote and can even be programmed. In addition, the 12 most important variables of each shot can be recorded. This makes the N90/F90 the ideal camera for documentation in science and research, in repro photography, for shooting a series of exposures in advertising, etc. Looked at in this light, the N90/F90 and Data Link that appeared to be too expensive at first glance suddenly have a good price/features ratio. You will find a detailed treatment of the possibilities of the Data Link in the special chapter Data Link and Electronic Organizer.

Operating the N90/F90

All functions and values are set by electronic impulses on the N90/F90. By pressing the appropriate function button and simultaneously turning the input control dial, the desired value can be set or the desired mode selected. The following chapter should quickly help you understand the functions of the N90/F90 in detail. Since you have spent a great deal of money on the N90/F90, it would be a shame to only make use of a small portion of its features. It would be best for you to use this chapter as a crash course and try everything immediately.

The Camera Body, Front

Let's examine the N90/F90 closely, with the lens removed. Top left, at the front edge of the handgrip, you will see a rectangular, red LED window which is the self-timer indicator. Top right, at the outside edge of the bayonet mount, you will find a black lug attached to a rotating ring. This is for the mechanical aperture transmitter, necessary when using non-AF lenses. Slightly below this is a white dot. Line this up with the white dot on your lens to correctly align the two. To its right are two screw caps. The upper cap conceals a Flash sync socket, and under the lower one is a 10-pin combined connector for Data Link and remote triggering. This connector is only compatible with the new cable release MC-20. In order to use the old MC-12A cable, the adapter cable MC-25 is required. Halfway up the camera body is the lens release button. The AF mode selector for focusing functions is located directly below it.

❒ **AF mode "M" (manual)** - For manual focusing. You can use the focus confirmation indicator in the viewfinder to aid in focusing lenses of f/5.6 or faster maximum aperture. PC-Nikkors, Reflex-Nikkors, and slower lenses can be focused manually by using the viewfinder.

❒ **AF mode "S" (single)** - Shown as "AF + F" on the LCD panel. This mode is based on sharpness priority. That is, even if the

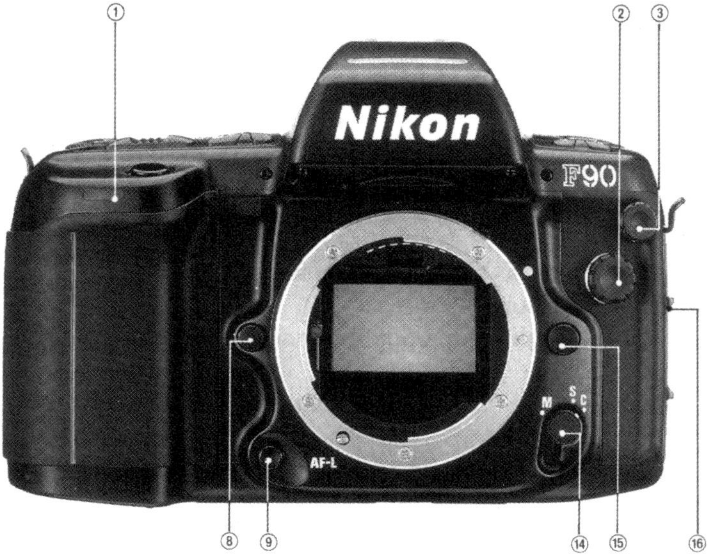
①
② ③
Nikon
F90
AF-L
M S C
⑧ ⑨ ⑭ ⑮ ⑯

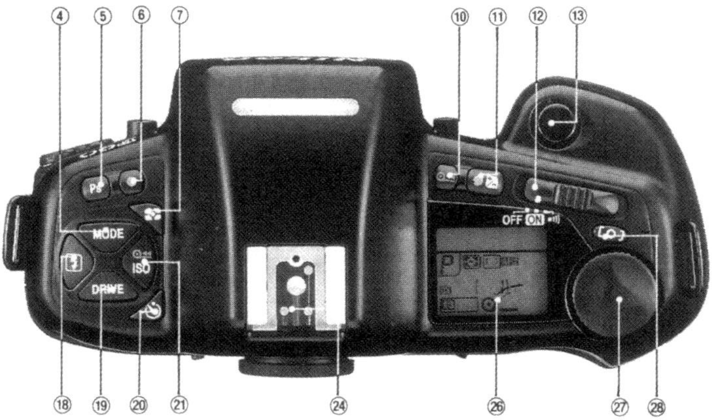
④ ⑤ ⑥ ⑦ ⑩ ⑪ ⑫ ⑬
MODE
ISO
DRIVE
OFF ON
⑱ ⑲ ⑳ ㉑ ㉔ ㉖ ㉗ ㉘

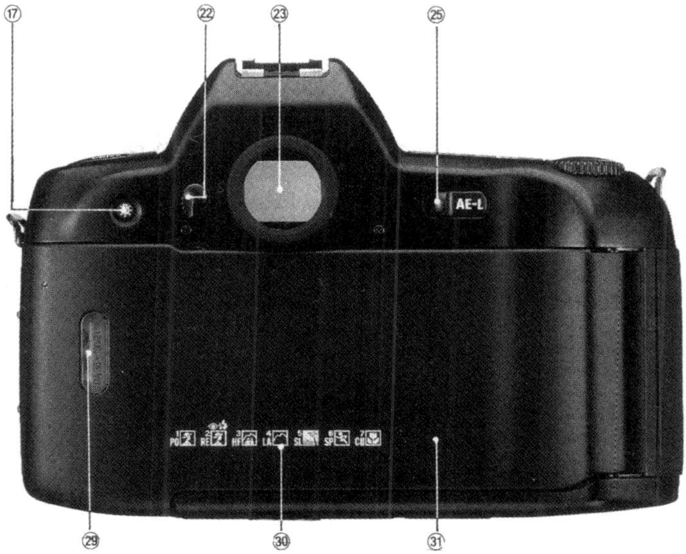

N90/F90 Operating Functions

1. Self-timer LED
2. 10-pin Remote Control Connector
3. Sync Connector
4. Exposure Mode Selector Button
5. Vari-program Button
6. Reset Button
7. Metering Mode Selector Button
8. Depth of Field Preview Button
9. AF Storage Button
10. Rewind Button
11. Exposure Compensation/ Reset Button
12. Main Power Switch
13. Shutter Release Button
14. AF Mode Selector
15. Lens Release Button
16. Camera Back Release
17. Viewfinder Illumination Button
18. Flash Sync Mode Button
19. Film Transport Mode Button
20. Self-timer Button
21. Film Speed/Rewind Button
22. Eyepiece Shutter
23. High-eyepoint Viewfinder
24. Accessory Shoe
25. Auto-exposure Lock Button
26. LCD Panel
27. Command Dial
28. AF Field Size Button
29. Film Cartridge Confirmation Window
30. Vari-program List
31. Camera Back

shutter release button is completely depressed, the shutter will only be released when the image is completely sharp.

❒ **Automatic focus lock in "S" mode -** Focus can be determined for a stationary object by touching the shutter release button and remains locked as long as the button is not released. The composition can therefore be changed without changing the focus. To expose, completely depress the shutter release button.

❒ **AF mode "C" (continuous) -** Displayed as AF + R in the LCD panel. This mode is based on exposure priority. As long as the shutter release button is partially depressed, the autofocusing system continually adjusts itself. When the button is completely depressed, an exposure will be made, even if the image happens not to be perfectly sharp. The disadvantage of "C" therefore, is the danger of out-of-focus pictures. The advantage is that the focus is constantly adjusted while panning.

❒ **Dynamic autofocus -** Both AF modes "S" and "C" use multiple lightning-fast measurements, one after the other, so that the distance of objects that are moving can be predicted at the time of exposure.

Lens Mount

Located inside the bayonet ring of the N90/F90, on the upper inside edge, are 7 contacts that electronically transmit lens variables. The lens ROM microchip transmits the values for maximum aperture, set aperture, focal length, and distance (only with type D Nikkors) to the camera. The camera's CPU uses these values to calculate the correct values for focusing and exposure. In the middle of the left inner edge of the camera, inside the bayonet, you will find the spring-loaded aperture lever. This lever sets the working aperture on the lens when an exposure is made. You will see a hole in the bottom left of the bayonet mount where the motor drive shaft for lens focusing connects to the lens. Be absolutely sure never to touch any of these extremely delicate components.

Located outside the bayonet ring on the left side is the depth of field preview button. When this button is depressed, the lens closes from wide open to the working aperture to enable visual confirmation of the depth of field in the viewfinder. However, this button may only be used in "A" and "M" modes. Below this, on the lower edge of the camera, you will find the AF-L Button. When depressed, the last focus setting is locked-in (useful in "C" mode).

Back

If you look from the back into the open camera, you will see the camera back locking mechanism on the far left and beside it, the film cassette bay. The slotted rewind shaft protrudes into this bay. On the right are the DX-contacts, which automatically read the DX-coded film speed off the film cassette. In the middle of the camera you can see the shutter blades. When loading and removing film, never touch these blades as they are very sensitive and can be easily damaged. To the right of the shutter, you can see the auto film loading mechanism. It consists of the film transport sprocket wheel and the take-up spool. The red markings on the bottom indicate how far the film has to be pulled out of its cassette to be loaded. Beside this on the camera back wall are the film guides and the film pressure plate. This plate is very sensitive and can easily be knocked out of alignment, resulting in poor film flatness and a loss of sharpness.

Top

At the top of the camera is the prism finder. With its high placement, the viewfinder can be used from a slight distance, thanks to specialized optics. This feature is very important for photographers who wear glasses. Also available for the eyepiece are corrected diopters, an eye cup, and a magnifier. On the left side of the eyepiece, you will see the eyepiece shutter lever. Still farther left is the LCD panel illumination button which turns the panel's lights on for about 8 seconds.

The auto-exposure lock lever is located to the right of the eyepiece. While this lever is pressed to the left and held, the exposure value that was last measured will be stored, in all exposure modes except "M." This value will be used for the next shot, even if the subject's illumination or contrast has changed after panning, for example. When the camera back is closed, you can always see if there is film loaded and its type by looking through the film cartridge confirmation window. On the standard camera back, there is a list of the Vari-program symbols.

On the left side, behind the button cluster, you will find the self-timer button. To set the self-timer, turn the command dial while pressing this button. Times are variable between 2 and 30 seconds. A second self-timer exposure can also be selected. This exposure will happen 10 seconds after the first (double self-timer).

To the top right of the cluster, you will find a button bearing the Matrix metering symbol. This button allows you select one of the three metering modes, by pressing it while turning the command dial.

- **Matrix -** Represented by a large rectangle divided into 5 segments.
- **Spot -** Represented by a small dot in a rectangle.
- **Center-weighted -** Represented by a dot in a circle, both within a larger rectangle.

The "PS" button is located on the front edge of the camera. This button controls the vari-progams, which should actually be called subject programs. There are seven such programs: 1) "Po"= Portrait. 2) "rE"= Portrait with flash and pre-flash. 3) "SL"= Silhouette. 4) "HF"= Maximum depth of field. 5) "LA"= Landscape. 6) "SP"= Sport. 7) "CU"= Close-up.

At the left side of the main switch and beside the LCD panel is the function key for manually selected exposure correction (+/- symbol). When this button is pressed, the set exposure correction value is displayed on the main LCD and in the viewfinder. The value can be changed by turning the command dial on the right side of the LCD. If the button is released after selecting a new value, the exposure correction symbol appears in both the main LCD and in the viewfinder (+/-). The numerical value of the correction is unfortunately still only displayed by pressing the +/- button on the N90/F90. The green dot on the +/- key indicates that this button doubles as the reset key release. If this button and the reset key (the green key on the other side of the viewfinder)

This conference scene resulted from reporting on a managers' summit. ⇨

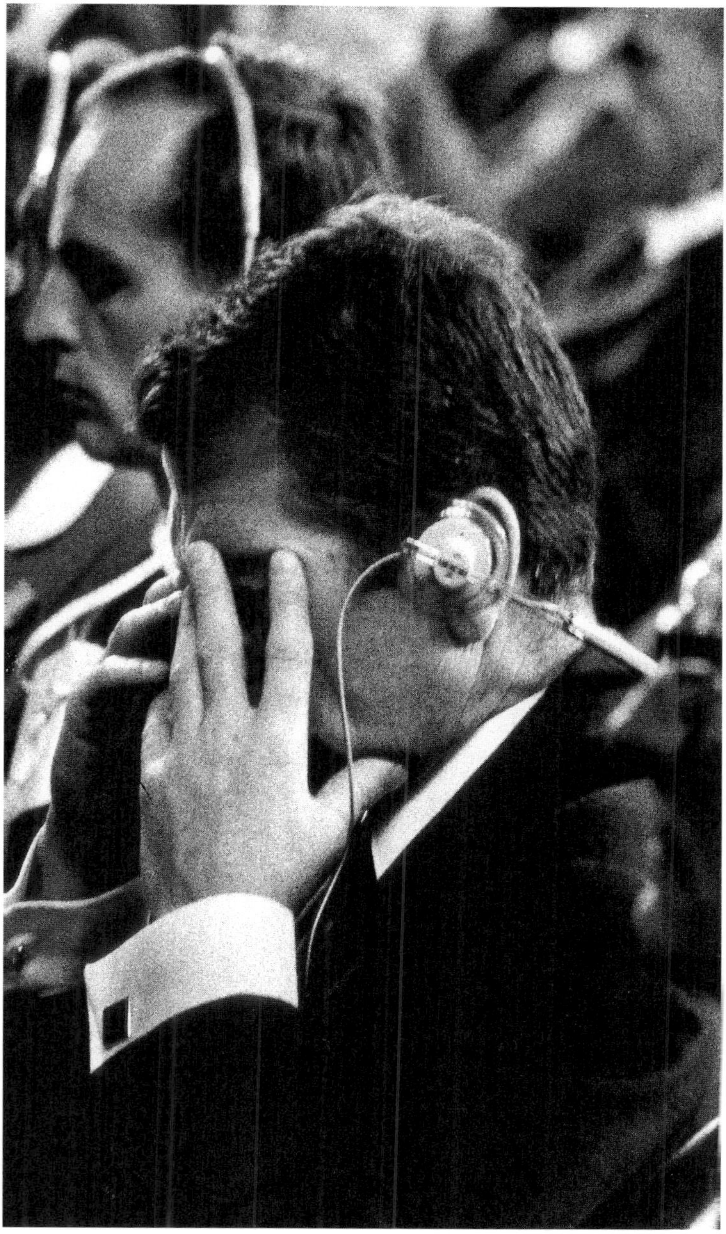

are pressed simultaneously for approximately 1 second, the camera resets to its default settings (program mode, Matrix metering, large autofocus field, and AF mode "S"). To the left of the reset button is the film rewind button, which is marked in red. When this button is pressed at the same time as the film rewind button (in the cross-shaped set of function keys on the other side of the viewfinder), the film will rewind.

On top of the viewfinder housing is the accessory shoe with the flash contacts. All of the flash functions from the N8008/F801 and F4 are possible with the Nikon SB-20, SB-22, SB-23, SB-24 flashes. A set of special N90/F90 functions are only possible with the SB-25, and some of these only with Nikkor type-D lenses.

LCD

The main LCD panel is located to the left of the command dial. All the actual values and functions are displayed simultaneously, while the LCD read-out in the viewfinder is limited to the most important information.

❒ **Top row -** Here, exposure values are displayed; on the left the exposure time (including B, under, and over-exposure warnings), and on the right the aperture (f-stop). This line is only active when the shutter release button is touched.

❒ **Second row -** Continuously displays the following from left to right: exposure mode (M, A, P), metering system, and the selected AF focusing area. Temporarily displayed is the AF mode (S,C,MF) and the flash modes (normal, with pre-flash, slow, and rear).

❒ **Third row -** Continuously displays the frame counter, ISO, exposure correction factor, self-timer duration, and the selected Vari-program, depending on which function key is touched. At the end of the row is a symbol for the connected Electronic Organizer and a display for programs entered via Data Link.

❒ **Bottom row -** A constant display of the motorized film advance mode (S, L, H). Beside this is a symbol which indicates if film is loaded and another which indicates film transport. If these symbols flash, the film is either torn or jammed. When the self-timer is activated, a clock symbol is displayed here. At the end of the row is the battery power indicator which is only active when the shutter release button is slightly depressed.

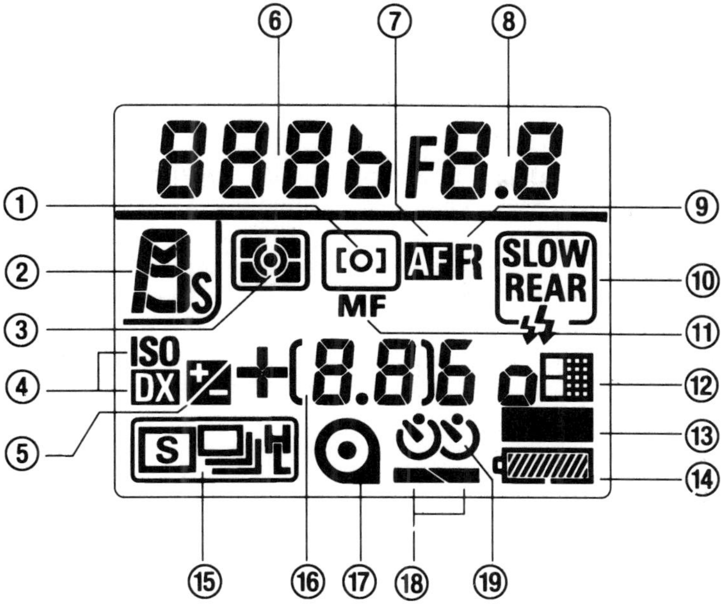

LCD Readout

1. Auto Focus Area
2. Exposure Mode
3. Metering Mode
4. ISO/DX Indicator
5. Exposure Compensation
6. Shutter Speed
7. Autofocus
8. Aperture
9. Release/Focus Priority
10. Flash Sync Mode/ Red Eye Priority
11. Manual Focus
12. Electronic Organizer *
13. Custom
14. Battery
15. Film Advance Mode
16. Frame-counter/ Vari-program/ISO Speed/ Self-timer Duration/Exposure Compensation Value
17. Film Loading
18. Film Advance and Rewind
19. Self-timer

** Appears only when Data Link System is un use.*

Button Cluster

On the left side of the viewfinder housing, where traditional cameras have their rewind knob, you will find the function button cluster that controls the camera's main functions.

❒ **MODE** - With this button, you can select the exposure mode with the command dial. "A" represents aperture priority; exposure time is automatically set according to the manually selected aperture.

"S" stands for shutter-priority. For a manually set shutter speed, the camera automatically selects the correct aperture.

"P" is a multi-program mode. Here, the camera selects both the shutter speed and aperture, depending on the focal length of the lens. The longer the focal length, the faster the shutter speed in order to prevent motion blur. In addition, it is possible to manually change the program: you can select an exposure-equal combination of shutter speed and aperture by turning the command dial. For example, if the LCD panel shows f/5.6 at 1/250, you can select f/4 at 1/500 to catch a moving subject, or select f/8 at 1/125 to increase depth of field with a stationary object. The program change is displayed by a blinking "P" on the LCD panel.

"M" stands for manual exposure. This means that the aperture can be selected on the lens' aperture ring and the exposure can be freely selected via the command dial. An evaluation of the exposure is shown in the viewfinder and on the LCD display on a bar graph in 1/3 stop increments.

❒ **ISO** - This button is used to set the film sensitivity, between ISO 6 and ISO 6400 or automatic DX (displayed on the LCD panel). To set, simultaneously press the ISO key and turn the command dial. It is necessary to manually set the film sensitivity if the film cartridge is not DX-coded or if you would like to deliberately under- or over-expose an entire roll of film (for example, set a higher film sensitivity and "push" the processing under poor lighting conditions). If DX is selected, the film sensitivity will be automatically set (between ISO 6 and ISO 6400) when using DX coded film canisters. The DX symbol will appear on the LCD panel along with the film sensitivity when film is loaded. It is advisable to check if the film sensitivity was read correctly every time you load a new roll, as an error could result from dirty or imperfect connections.

This picture is the result of a documentary assignment about children in Rio de Janeiro. Additional photos from this location can be found elsewhere in this book ➪

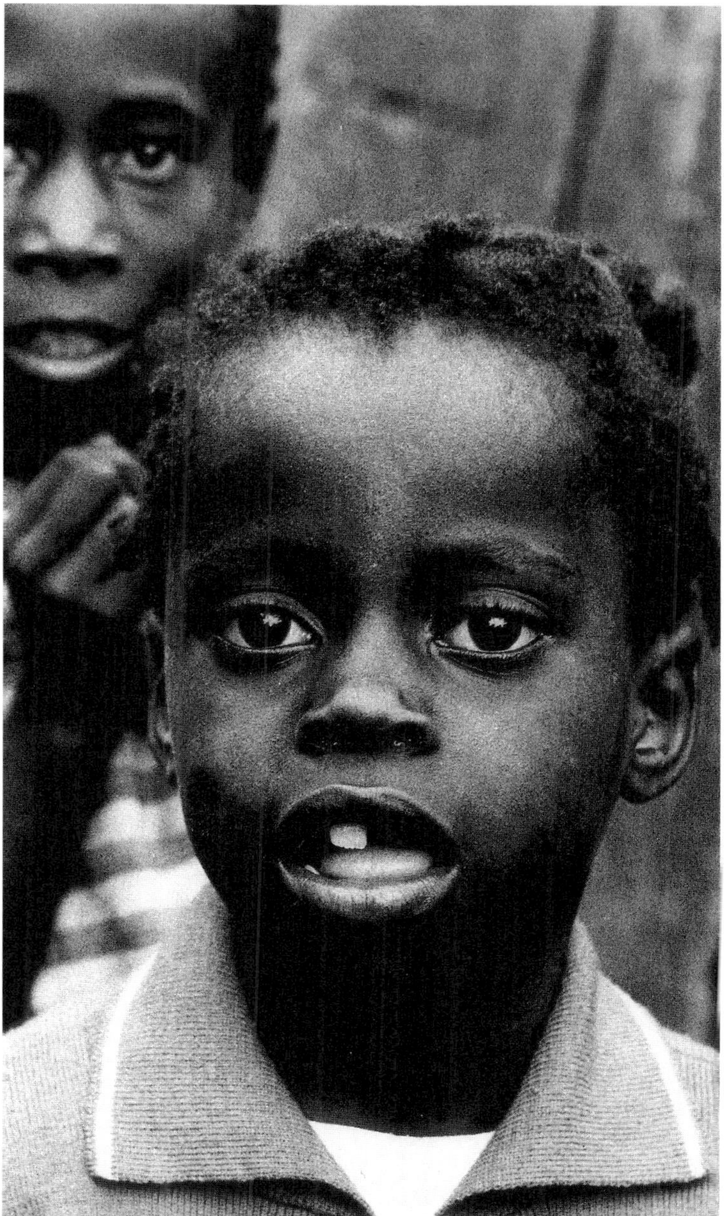

The film sensitivity button, identified by red markings, has a double function. When pressed at the same time as the rewind release button, it also acts as the film rewind key.

❐ **DRIVE** - The motorized film transport settings can be selected using the DRIVE key and the command dial. "S" stands for "single" and allows one exposure per depression of the shutter release button.

"L" represents slow continuous shooting. In this mode, as long as the shutter release button is held down, the camera will expose approximately 2 frames per second.

"H" represents high speed continuous shooting. In this mode, as long as the shutter release button is held, the camera will expose approximately 3.6 frames per second.

These per second values are valid for shutter speeds faster than 1/250 second, normal temperatures, and fresh batteries. Thanks to dynamic autofocus tracking, it is possible to have intervals between exposures fast enough to enable shooting 3.6 frames per second in autofocus mode. It is not possible to expose faster since the camera would not have enough time to focus. An exposure would not be made in AF mode "S," and an out-of-focus exposure would be taken in AF mode "C."

❐ **FLASH** - The button at the far left of the cluster is the flash button. This allows the user to switch between the many flash functions of the N90/F90. The normal setting is the simple flash symbol. In conjunction with spot metering or center-weighted metering and AF Nikkors, this represents Multi-Sensor TTL flash mode. In conjunction with Matrix metering, the camera automatically considers ambient light and contrast and produces a finely balanced fill-flash that even considers the distance to the subject when using D lenses (3D Multi-Sensor flash mode).

The setting depicted by the two flash symbols generates a pre-flash to prevent against red-eye and squinting. This option is available in all metering and exposure modes only when using the SB-25 flash.

Reflections in water often create an interesting combination of shape and color. To increase contrast and color, the original slide was duplicated by intentionally underexposing standard transparency film. Picture: Wolf Huber. ⇨

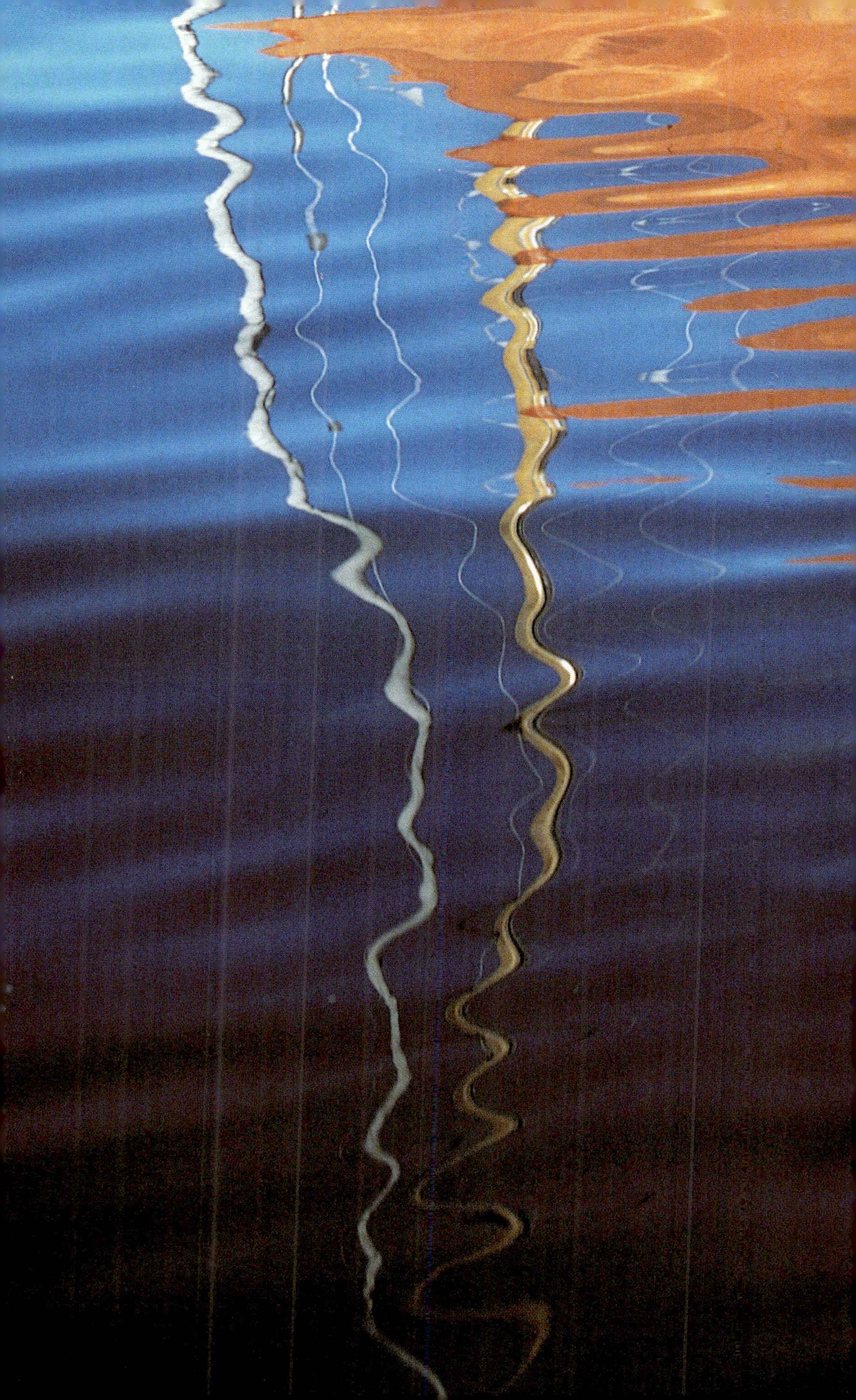

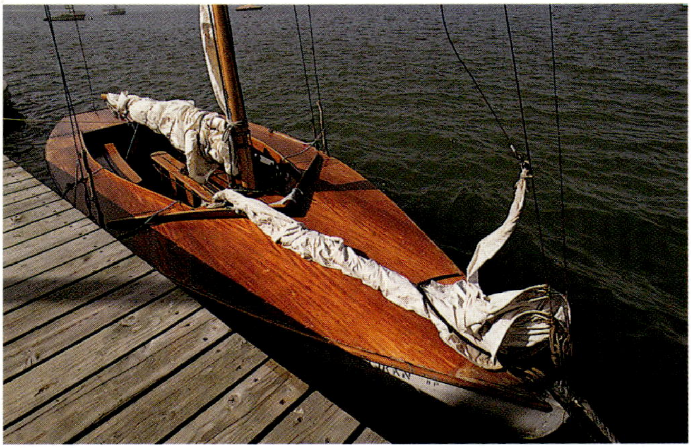

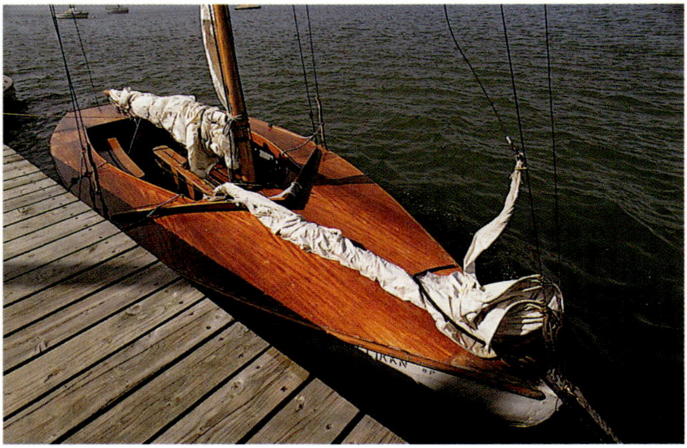

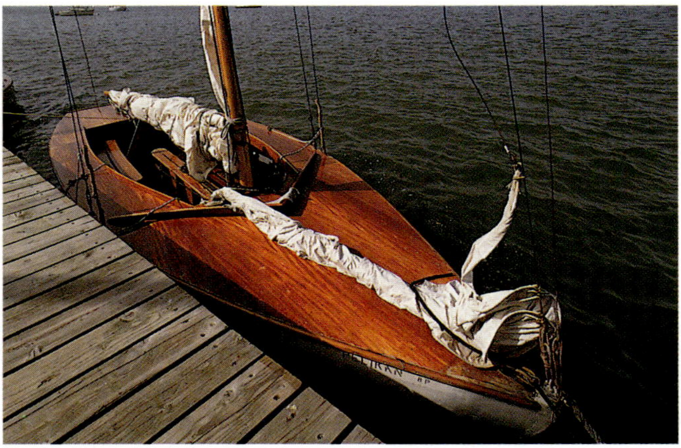

The next setting is the Slow flash function, represented by "SLOW" in the LCD panel. Using normal flash sync, the exposure modes "A" and "P" will select shutter speeds between 1/60 and 1/250 second, depending on the available light. "SLOW" increases the shutter speed time up to 30 seconds (basically permitting ambient light exposures of dark backgrounds).

The "REAR" setting synchronizes the flash with the second shutter blade. The flash will be triggered at the end of a long exposure and not at the beginning, as is usual. This way, motion blur is much more natural in that it appears to follow behind the moving object and not precede it as when the flash syncs with the first shutter curtain. In exposure modes "A" and "P," flash synchronization will be automatically switched to "SLOW," since "REAR" does not make sense when shutter speeds are 1/60 second or faster. On the SB-24 and SB-25, this function is selected on the flash unit itself.

Hand-grip

At the front right on the hand-grip is the shutter release button (no cable release thread). This release is a multi-function button: touching it very gently turns on the exposure electronics, pressing it slightly harder activates the autofocus systems, and completely depressing the button exposes the film and automatically advances it to the next frame. The camera's main power switch is behind this button, on the right. When the main switch is all the way to the right, the electronic beeper is activated. Directly behind this, you will find the focus area button which allows you to switch from large to small autofocus areas. On the back edge of the grip is the command dial. By simultaneously pressing a function key and turning this dial, you can change the value or mode of that function. For example, if the MODE button is depressed, you can change the exposure mode by turning the command dial.

Good results can be obtained using spot metering (top), center-weighted metering (middle), and Matrix metering (bottom).

The battery compartment lid is located on the underside of the camera at the bottom of the hand-grip. Located in the middle of the base plate on the lens axis is the 1/4″-20 tripod mounting socket. The serial number of the camera is also engraved on the bottom.

Viewfinder

If you look into the viewfinder, we see a small circle that represents the small autofocus field as well as the spot metering area. The larger rectangle represents the large AF field. (This

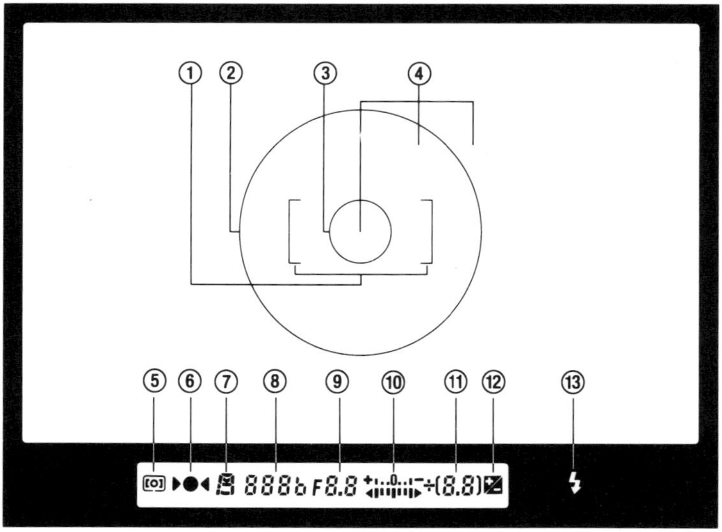

Viewfinder Display

1. Large AF Field
2. Center-weighted Measuring Field
3. Spot Metering Measuring Field
4. Groundglass
5. Selected AF Field
6. Sharpness Indicator
7. Exposure Mode
8. Shutter Speed
9. Working Aperture
10. Electronic Analog Display
11. Frame Counter/Selected Vari-program/Compensation Factor
12. Compensation Mark
13. Flash Needed/Flash Ready

central area contained by these two symbols approximates the three central exposure metering fields of 3D Matrix metering.) The large central circle indicates both the 75% weighting of center-weighted metering and the central metering area when the N90/F90 is in Matrix mode. When the shutter release button is touched lightly, the green back-lit LCD array appears. It, as well as the central LCD panel, stays on for approximately 8 seconds after the shutter button is released.

The AF area size is shown at the far left hand side of the viewfinder display. Beside it is the AF sharpness indicator (arrows and dot), followed by the selected exposure mode and the actual shutter speed and aperture. Exposure times and apertures are rounded to the nearest whole number on the display. The camera does use fractional values for internal calculations, however. An additional bar graph display appropriate to the mode appears beside this. In mode "M" it is a light scale, but it becomes an indicator for under- or over-exposure in "A" and "S" modes. At approximately the same spot, an indicator for over-exposure (HI) or under-exposure (LO) appears in all auto modes. The frame number is usually displayed at the far right of the viewfinder LCD. When an exposure correction is necessary, a +/- symbol along with the correction factor appears instead. The flash symbol LED is located on the right side of the LCD window. It glows green when flash is suggested or necessary based on ambient light conditions. The LED is red when the flash is charged and ready and blinks or goes out while the flash is recharging.

N90/F90: For Professionals, Hobbyists or Techno-Wizards?

Like the F4, the N90/F90 offers limited use of non-AF Nikkors in manual and aperture preferred modes as well as unlimited use of the complete AF Nikkor series. A unique feature of the N90/F90 is that it is compatible with all the functions of the AF-I Nikkors, like the F4, but is also compatible with the new Type D lenses. The N90/F90's fully electronic operation is particularly easy to use, like the N8008s. All important functions can be controlled without having to put the camera down. In comparison with the N8008s and the F4 with its Multi-function Back, the N90/F90 together with the Multi-function Back MF-26 offers the most photographically useful functions to date. Less important are the N90/F90's subject-specific programs, at least from a professional's point of view. In contrast, the N90/F90's many flash modes are of great importance to all levels of photographers. As with every fully electronic camera, however, one may not expect the N90/F90 to be as rugged as a good manual camera. This concern is not unfounded. Static, persistent humidity, salt water mist, etc. can lead to the occasional disappointment.

For the advanced amateur, the N90/F90 is probably the "Dream Nikon" with which he or she will be better served than with an F4. For the pro, it is the ideal complement to the F4 since the new D lenses and the rationalizing and automating functions of the Data Link can be used with the N90/F90. If one recognizes the possibilities of the N90/F90's Data Link for remote display, remote control and automatic storage of exposure data, this is the most versatile and powerful camera for documentation in research, development, and science to date. As the computer becomes more and more a necessary tool for the photographer, the N90/F90 can be profitably used as a data communication device in photographic training.

Basic Functions of the N90/F90

Power Supply and Battery Replacement

The electrical power supply must deliver power for the film transport, the shutter, cocking the reflex mirror springs, cocking the automatic diaphragm spring, as well as for metering and the autofocus drive motor. With such a camera, nothing works without batteries. Instead of the expensive and short lived sealed cells, Nikon uses inexpensive AA cells which are available worldwide.
❐ **Alkaline cells -** The 6v lithium sealed cell has 60% of the power of 4 fresh AA alkalines and costs about 2.5 times as much. In addition, it is not available everywhere. The lithium cell does have some advantages, however. It is smaller, lighter, has a long life, and loses very little energy during prolonged storage prior to use (about a 10% loss in 10 years). But how many advanced amateurs or pros leave their camera(s) sitting around unused for months?

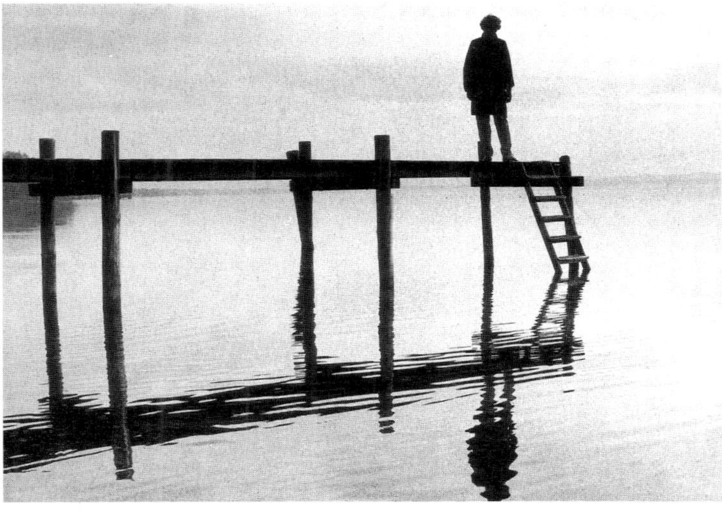

Even without using the silhouette program, this type of picture is possible when using center-weighted metering.

Therefore, the AA cells, available in every corner store or supermarket, are, without question, the most professional energy supply. Modern alkaline batteries are also mercury-free (make sure when you buy) and can be disposed of with other household garbage.

❒ **Carbon-Zinc batteries -** These are even cheaper than alkalines, but have less power, short shelf life, and are not good at low temperatures. They do not contain mercury.

❒ **NiCd batteries -** Only fully charged nickel-cadmium batteries can be used. Since NiCds discharge internally more rapidly than alkaline batteries, they are not necessarily recommended. On the other hand, modern NiCds can be recharged up to 1000 times with a good charger and are therefore very economical and environmentally preferred. A charger with a discharge device (refresher) should be used, especially with sporadic use of the camera. Damaged NiCds should not be disposed of with regular garbage or thrown into a fire.

❒ **External battery unit DB6 -** with 6 alkaline D cells, the capacity is 10 times that of the AA battery set. In addition, the operation in low temperatures is better.

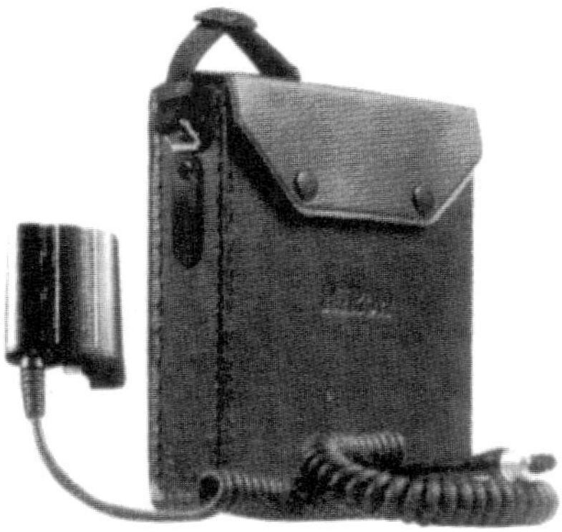

External battery DB-6.

Battery Drain

A brand new set of alkaline batteries lasts for about 75 rolls of 36 exposure film and for about 12 rolls at 14°F(-10°C). With carbon-zinc batteries, only 20 rolls of 36 exposure film can be used at 68°F(20°C). and at lower temperatures, these batteries are practically useless. With NiCds, you get about 55 rolls at

68°F(20°C) and 20 rolls at 14°F(-10°C). In my practical tests at normal temperatures and with lots of playing around with the autofocus, I was able to expose 20 rolls with the alkaline batteries.

Battery Power When it's Cold

The biggest enemy of batteries is low temperatures. Here only new "warm" alkaline batteries or freshly charged NiCd batteries help. Otherwise, the use of the DB-6 is necessary.

Battery Testing

The working voltage of the camera is 6 volts. As long as there is enough power for the motors, there is always plenty left for exposure and focus readings. Poorly exposed or out-of-focus pictures as a result of battery failure are therefore impossible. (My tests indicate that the camera quits when the voltage drops to 5.4v.) With new batteries, auto-shutoff of the LCD panel is in 8 seconds. With batteries that are just about dead, the camera shuts off in 2

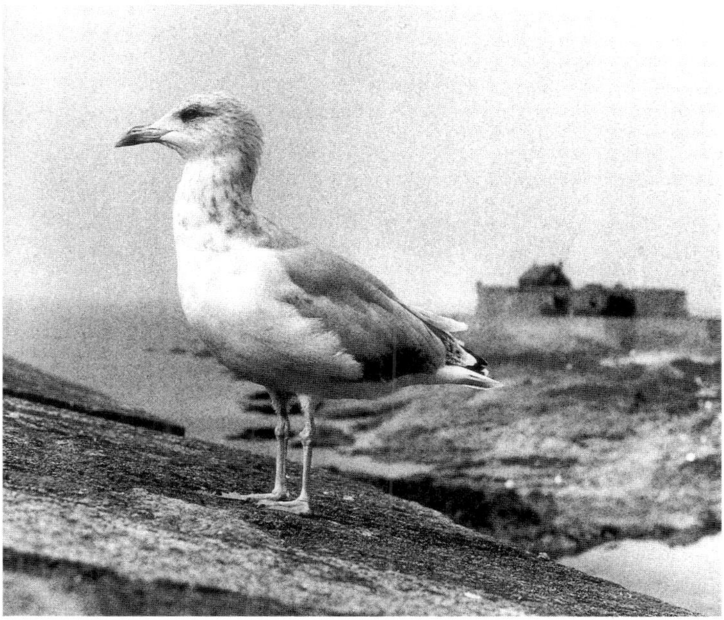

A focal length of at least 180mm, a shutter speed of 1/250 second, and a steady hand are necessary for this shot.

seconds. If the indicator turns off faster, or starts blinking, you should try a new set of batteries. The N90/F90 also has a battery condition indicator. If the battery symbol is no longer complete, you know it is best to keep a new set of batteries ready.

Battery Tips

Always keep a set of fresh batteries in reserve. In winter time, keep them warm in your trouser pockets. In case you do not expect to use your camera for a long period, take the batteries out of your camera to prevent damage due to leakage.

Film Handling

Obviously, a camera without film is as good as no camera at all. While the following may seem rudimentary, it is extremely important and should be reviewed.

❐ **Loading -** Insert the film cassette from the bottom into the film compartment and ensure that the rewind prongs engage the cassette spool. Now, hold the cassette in the camera with you left thumb and gently pull the film out to the red mark with your right hand. Ensure that the teeth of the film sprocket line up with the perforations in the film. Close the camera back, press the shutter release button once, and the film will automatically be transported to picture number 1.

❐ **Possible errors -** Trouble can only occur if the film was pulled out too far (or not far enough) during loading. Judging from the number of rolls of film I have loaded into the N90/F90, I can safely state that 1/16th inch more or less makes no difference. If you are not sure that the film was loaded correctly, simply look at the film counter on the LCD panel. The film transport is electronically checked and only actual film movement is counted. If the film is not properly inserted, jams, or is torn, the LCD panel will show a blinking film transport symbol and you will hear a beeping sound.

❐ **Rewinding -** If the end of the film has been reached, you will see the word "END" on the LCD panel and the camera will not fire. When the rewind button and the rewind locking button are pressed simultaneously, the rewind motor is activated and the film winds back into the cassette (the counter counts backwards). When the film end is reached, the counter and the film transport checker on the LCD panel indicate empty ("E") and the rewind motor switches off.

The N90/F90 rewinds the film completely into the cassette, including the lead portion. I personally find that this feature has more advantages than disadvantages. For example, you can never confuse an exposed film with an unexposed film, even in moments of high pressure. Additionally, film that is completely rewound cannot be pulled out rapidly at the processing lab. A film end that sticks out may be helpful for a darkroom technician, but pulling the film out of the cassette can cause scratches, sparks and dust -attracting electro-static charges. With high speed films from ISO 1000 and faster, light could enter through the slit in the cassette of a completely rewound film and slightly fog the first few frames. You should tape the slit shut with black tape right after taking the cassette out of the camera or wrap the whole cassette in tin foil. Both methods worked well in my photographic experience. By the way, several companies sell gadgets that can retrieve the film end out of the cassette, should it be necessary.

The rewinding process can only be interrupted by opening the camera back. If you look at the film counter, you can rewind partially exposed film such that the leading end still sticks out. You can also have your camera reprogrammed by Nikon service so that the film only rewinds up to the leader.

Film Speed

Like most camera manufacturers, Nikon does not indicate old ASA or DIN values. Both have been switched ISO values.

❐ **Manual adjustment -** Hold the ISO button down and you can set the film speed from ISO 6 to ISO 6400 by turning the command dial. If you want to under- or over-expose a whole roll of film by deliberately changing the film speed, you should set the speed manually. Also, sometimes the film speed indicated by the manufacturer is not right for you and a manual film speed setting is necessary. If you attempt to correct using the camera's exposure system, you could get confused if you also have to correct with respect to the subject.

❐ **Automatic DX -** Turn the command dial until the DX symbol appears in the LCD. DX-coded films will automatically be recognized. Most film cassettes are imprinted with coded information that can be read by machines. By alternatively reading blank metal (conductive) and a printed surface (non-conductive), the camera picks up the code with electrical contacts and transmits this film speed code directly into the electronic exposure system.

If an uncoded cartridge is loaded, the camera blocks the release buttons and shows a blinking DX, ERR and ISO on the LCD panel. Wrong exposures are therefore impossible; you simply have to set the film speed manually.

If you take a film out of a refrigerator and load it into your camera, the condensation on the outside of the cassette can confuse the DX contacts. The same effect can happen if you touch the cassette with sweaty or dirty hands. In the worst of all cases, the DX system will read the cartridge incorrectly and a wrong film speed will be set without warning. This is why I make a habit of double-checking the ISO setting at the start of every roll by pressing the ISO button.

Motorized Film Transport

If the autofocus system of the N90/F90 detects moving objects, it will automatically switch to continuous film transport if the AF mode is set at "C." In this case, the N90/F90 will transport the film in either "L" or "C" setting at a maximum speed of 3 frames per second.

❐ **Advantages -** It does not matter if you shoot a wedding party leaving a church, a soccer game, or children playing. You do not have to take the camera away from your eye to advance the film. You therefore keep aiming at the subject and the number of good pictures increases. Selecting "S," "L," or "H" mode depends on the subject. The more hectic the situation, the more reason to switch to continuous transport mode.

Motorized film transport is also of great help for copy work or close-ups with a tripod. A manual film transport would constantly move the carefully positioned camera out of place. In order to keep camera shake to a minimum, you should work with a remote release or self-timer. The best remotely triggered exposures are really only possible with motorized film transport. This is, by the way, the main reason why I now personally support the motorized film transport system.

❐ **Disadvantage -** As a photographer educated in manual photography, I could never deny some misgivings about winders and motor drives in spite of years of working with motorized film transport. The motor drive is just too noisy to permit undetected shooting. However, to a certain extent, this disadvantage can be compensated for.

Viewfinder System

High-eyepoint Viewfinder

The N90/F90's viewfinder is the same as that found on the N8008s and is therefore the very best available. In addition to its eyeglass-friendly design, it is home to several other important features.

❒ **Eyepiece shutter -** The built-in eyepiece shutter of the N90/F90 prevents stray light from entering the viewfinder, where it could adversely influence the light meter reading. This is indispensable for long exposures in automatic mode when the eye is away from the eyepiece.

❒ **Interchangeable focusing screens -** The bright clear focusing screen is outstanding. The particularly even and fine-grained surface finish permits focusing even under low light conditions or with slow lenses. The N90/F90 comes with the universal focusing screen type B which can be exchanged with a screen that has a grid of horizontal and vertical lines. This screen is recommended for constant use by professionals since it is always useful whether one wants to judge converging lines, line up original prints or check magnification scales. Another useful viewer accessory for people with slight eye problems are the corrected diopters. Personally, I feel it is more practical to keep wearing my glasses.

The high-magnification finder DG-2 (with the adapter DK-7) is probably only used by fans of macro photography.

❒ **Shutter -** The N90/F90 shutter is a vertically travelling, electrically triggered, electronically controlled, metal focal plane shutter made of a wear-resistant metal alloy.

Because of its lightweight design, this shutter is capable of speeds from 30 seconds to 1/8000 second. With the high speed sync setting "FP," it is possible to take flash pictures with speeds up to 1/4000 second. Additionally, the photographer can use fast shutter speeds together with large apertures and fill flash to separate the subject from the background.

Camera Trouble

When the N90/F90 will not function, there are several possible causes. You may need new batteries, have forgotten to load a roll of film, or may be using an unsuitable lens. Mistakes like these can happen to anyone in hectic situations. In these cases the N90/F90 diagnoses and indicates the mistakes for you. The situation is different if the photographer gets confused with the multitude of camera functions or if the camera itself stops working due to overload.

❒ **Reset button** - If you cannot figure out what's wrong, the best solution may be the reset button. To reset the N90/F90, simultaneously press both of the green reset buttons. The camera will return to its basic functions.

The reset buttons of the N90/F90 can also be used to activate or deactivate the functions of Data-Link (for more information on the Data-Link, please refer to to that section).

❒ **Overload warning** - If the N90/F90's shutter does not release, LCD panel blinks meaninglessly, mode cannot be changed, main power switch does not operate, or mirror does not spring back, there may be an overload.

❒ **Causes** - Several causes are possible, among them slightly jammed film and electrostatic charges. Problems caused by incompatible lenses or bad batteries are not considered overloads.

❒ **Remedy** - Switch the camera off and remove the batteries for several minutes. The overloaded micro-computer will discharge itself and should become operational again.

If this type of problem happens frequently, a chip might actually be damaged. In this case, take the camera to your nearest authorized Nikon dealer.

Automatic and Manual Focusing with the N90/F90

The N90/F90's focusing options can be selected using the three-position selector switch.

Taking Pictures in AF Mode

Select the AF mode and the AF field size, aim at your subject and press the shutter release half-way. When the in-focus symbol (round black dot) appears in the viewfinder, you can fully depress the trigger and be guaranteed a sharp picture.

Keep in mind that every automation is only as good as its application. Contrary to manual focusing, which is instinctive for the experienced photographer, autofocus demands a deliberate decision. Only when the photographer knows exactly which area of the subject should be in focus can he aim precisely. After that, however, the autofocus mechanism quickly takes care of the rest.

Two Autofocus Field Sizes

The N90/F90 makes available two, different-sized AF measuring fields. There is no rule as to which one is better in a given situation. It depends on the specific subject and the methods of the photographer.

❒ **Small area -** In my experience, selecting the smaller field is safer when the subject has a complicated structure. If the focal point of a large, deep subject should be at a specific distance, then a selected edge can be accurately pin-pointed with the small field. With the large area, other subject areas will be included and it is questionable where the effective focus setting will end up. Normally, focusing with the small area takes a bit longer, a fact that could be very annoying in hectic situations. Use it for specially selected settings such as portraits, landscapes, and architectural pictures

❒ **Large area -** The advantage of the large AF field is that there is a good chance that an edge of almost any subject will be selected for the camera to focus on. The large AF field is therefore ideal for all types of action shots, always bearing in mind that there is the chance that the desired subject detail may not be in focus. Use it for relaxed coverage of exhibitions or slow sports events.

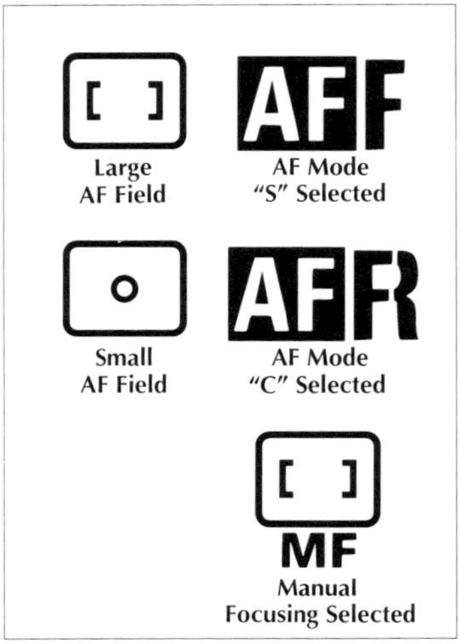

Focus Priority

In the AF mode "S," the N90/F90 always uses focus priority. In other words, the automatic focusing precedes the shutter release. As long as the autofocus system has not selected a focus setting, the shutter cannot be released. It is the other way around with the "C" mode. Here the shutter release takes precedence over focusing.

Focus Anticipation

The AF system of the N90/F90 measures the distance twice in both modes before it adjusts the focus and calculates the distance of the moving subject at the time of shutter release. This AF control works with an anticipated focus setting or calculation.

Continuous Servo Focusing

If, with the AF mode "C" the shutter release button is only slightly depressed, the N90/F90's autofocus continuously corrects focus. That is, after each focus adjustment, it immediately takes the next two readings and refocuses if necessary. Therefore, with moving subjects or panning, the focus is continuously adjusted. This is also called autofocus tracking.

Automatic Focus Storage

In "S" mode, you can get a sharp image using autofocus even if your subject is not in the AF field. First, aim the camera so that the subject is at the center of the frame, then partially depress the shutter release button until the viewfinder display shows the in-focus symbol. The focus distance will remain unchanged as long as the trigger is held in the half-depressed position. The subject can now be moved anywhere in the frame before exposure.

If you decide not to take the picture after all and want to focus on another subject, simply release the shutter button. The stored distance setting will be automatically cleared. Depressing the shutter release again restarts the whole process.

AF-L button

This is used to store a selected focusing distance.

❒ **In AF mode "C"** - If, after aiming and focusing in AF mode "C," you press the AF lock button, the focus setting will remain constant. As long as you keep the AF-L button depressed, you can take as many pictures as you like with this stored distance setting.

❒ **In AF mode "S"** - In this mode, stored focus information is cancelled after each exposure. If, however, after focusing on a specific subject detail, you release the shutter button and press the AF-L button, the N90/F90 will switch to shutter release priority. As long as the AF-L button is depressed, you can take as many pictures as you like with the stored focus information.

Long-term AF Storage

If you wish to take several pictures of a subject at a constant distance but at longer time intervals, then a long term storage of the focus distance setting is best. After focusing in AF mode "S," release the shutter button and switch to AF mode "M." The selected focus setting remains constant as long as you like.

Long-term Distance Storage

In either AF mode "S" or "C," you can photograph any given subject with pre-selected focus and exposure. In AF mode "S," simply use the AE-L slide-switch after focusing, and while pressing lightly on the shutter release button. In AF mode "C" with the Camera Back MF-26 or Data Back, exposure and focusing distance are stored by simply pressing the AF-L button.

AF with Flash Assistance

If there is not enough light, not only does the autofocus system fail, but also the human eye. In this case, the use of Nikon autofocus flash units SB-20, SB-22, SB-23, SB-24 or SB-25 is helpful.

❒ **In total darkness** - In addition to the regular flash possibilities, these flash units contain a special infrared AF illuminator. In other words, if you set the N90/F90 to AF mode "S" and depress the shutter release button, whenever there is not enough light for the operation of the AF system, the flash will transmit infrared light for as long as it takes the AF system to focus. The visible portion of the near-infrared beam is bright enough to be seen up to about 20 feet.If you take a picture now, you are guaranteed to get a sharp flash picture. After focusing with the pulsing infrared beam, you can also store the distance by gently pressing down on the shutter release button or the AF-L switch and then turning the flash off. If you then select AF mode "M," you can take available light pictures with the stored setting.

❒ **On low-contrast subjects -** The emitted infrared beam permits focusing on low-contrast subjects by giving the N90/F90's autofocusing system something other than a monochromatic surface to work with.

Limits of Autofocusing

The autofocus system of the N90/F90 reads distance indirectly. That means that the subject is scanned from the image projected by the camera lens, and from this, the camera's computer will calculate the necessary movement of the lens. After all, the automatic focusing depends on the reading and evaluation of picture contrast, and that in turn means that the subject has to have some contrast and the projected image from the camera's lens cannot be too dark.

Autofocusing Requirements

For the N90/F90's AF system to function properly, several requirements must be met.

❒ **Lens selection -** Slow lenses are useless for AF photography. The AF system needs a relatively strong light beam to recognize sharpness. With small apertures, the edges of the light transmission are cut off and the light beam is too narrow. For the N90/F90, the lens must be f/5.6 or faster. Additionally, the AF setting doesn't work well with very short focal lengths. The AF is confused due to the

These architectural details from the Saracenic period demand the greatest care, particularly when enlarging. Careful selection enlarging paper grades is essential. ⇨

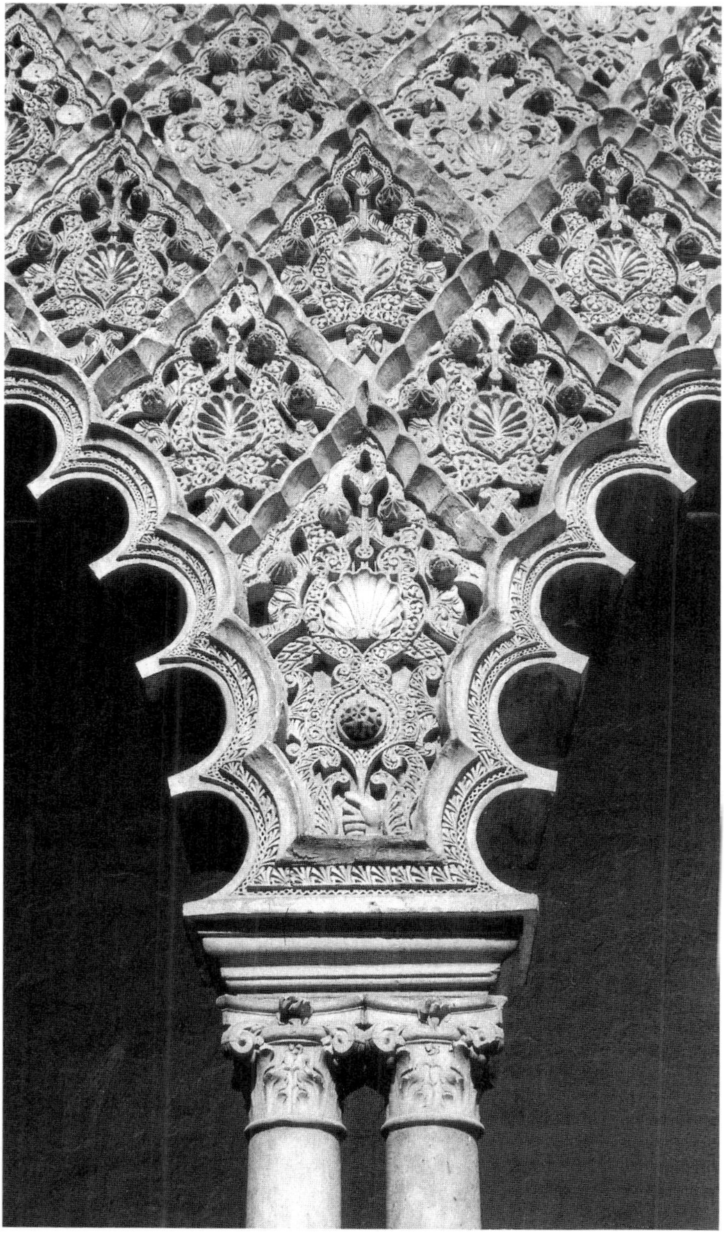

large depth of field of extreme wide angles. Even in these cases, there is an optimum focus distance, but the AF has difficulty finding it. This is similar to a photographer who, if he is not sure, sets the distance on the distance scale rather than trusting his eyes.

❐ **Object brightness** - The autofocusing system has problems with subjects darker than EV 1 (approximately candlelight). At this light level, even manual focusing is almost impossible. Use a Nikon flash in these situations.

❐ **Subject contrast** - Another difficult situation arises with low contrast subjects. Normally the AF mechanism of the lens will focus from close-up to infinity, and then the AF symbol will appear in the viewfinder display.

❐ **Subject structure** - If the structure of an otherwise contrasty subject is too small, the autofocus system can fail. For instance, try focusing on the small black type of a newspaper. In contrast to the old AF sensors, the crossfield sensor of the N90/F90 does not differentiate between the horizontal or vertical orientation of a structure. The AF system of the N90/F90 has no more problems whether the structures are vertical, on angle or horizontal.

❐ **Strong backlight** - Extremely backlit situations or highly reflective objects can, due to their brightness, lower the contrast in the AF field to a point where AF is no longer possible. These situations are very rare.

❐ **Difficult to define subjects** - Here we are talking about various subjects at different distances. An example is two children standing behind each other where the face of the child in front is in one AF segment and the child farther away in another. Which child should the camera focus on? My practical experience with the camera shows that it normally selects the front subject. Sometimes this can be annoying, as in shooting through a wire fence, wanting the scene behind the fence to be in focus. In these cases you should, if possible, fill the focus brackets in the viewfinder with your subject, then lock the focus, recompose, and shoot the desired scene. If this still does not work, you can always resort to manual focusing.

❐ **Filters and creative lens attachments** - There are 3 situations which make it difficult or impossible for the AF system to work: 1) You can take too much light away and thereby lower the light transmission of your lens (e.g. color filters, graduated filters, vignettes, etc.). There is nothing to worry about with UV or skylight filters. 2) You can reduce the contrast too much (e.g. soft focus or fog filters). 3) You can polarize the light and confuse the AF sensor that is sensitive to linear polarized light. Only circular polarizers should be used with autofocus cameras.

The Verdict on Autofocusing

Subjects and situations where AF does not work do not necessarily detract from the many advantages inherent to autofocus photography. After all, even a human can only see objects if they are bright enough and if the outlines or details are clearly defined.

Manual Focusing

With unsuitable subjects or slow lenses that cannot be used with autofocus, you must focus by eye.

In the manual focus mode "M", you have to focus in the conventional way by turning the focusing ring of the lens by hand. This mode also works with non-AF lenses.

With lenses faster than f/5.6, the AF system comes to your assistance. The AF indicator in the viewfinder displays which way the lens has to be turned and when focus has been reached by displaying arrows or a circle in the viewfinder.

Autofocusing: How Does it Work

The AF system of the N90/F90, simply stated, consists of 4 building blocks. The first is the ROM microchip in the lens, which transmits vital information such as brightness, selected focal length, actual aperture, and distance setting via the contacts inside the bayonet mount.

Inside the camera is the AF module (AF-IC). This semiconductor CCD array consists of 172 horizontal and 72 vertical CCD's in a cross formation. Two closely timed sets of information from these CCD's are interpreted by an integrated circuit and the result is passed on to the camera's CPU. The computer then calculates the two successive distance values and determines (with moving objects) the estimated distance at the time of the shutter release. This estimated distance is then calculated with the lens data to establish an electronic command for the autofocus motor. The AF motor IC then passes this information to the motor itself in

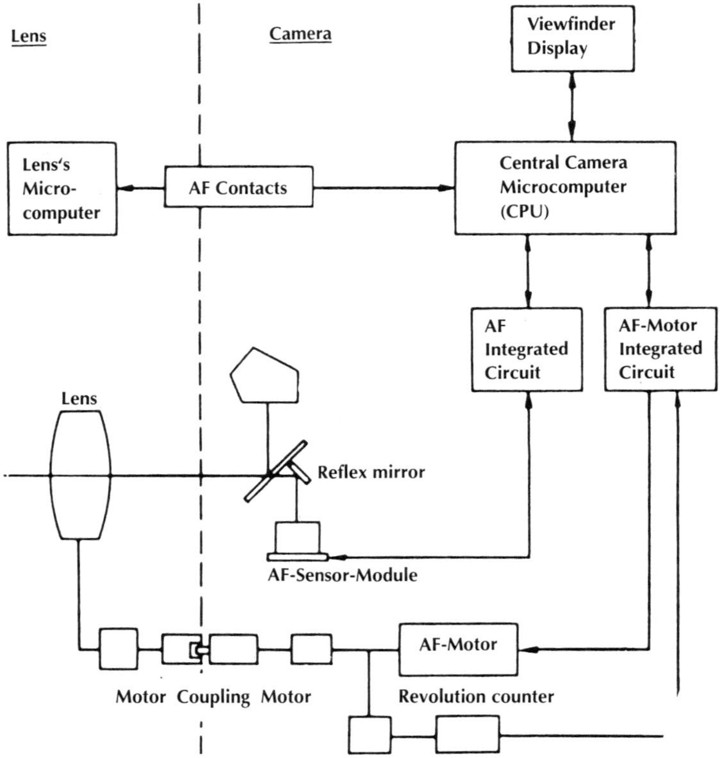

Autofocus Operation Flowchart

Top: Manual exposure set for the background (f/8 at 1/250 second) was enhanced by using SB-25 fill-flash for the foreground. The result was a well-balanced picture.
Bottom: With ISO 400 film and aperture priority in SLOW flash mode (f/5.6 at 1/15 second). Using fill-flash results in a good compromise between sharp flash exposure and the motion effect of a time exposure.

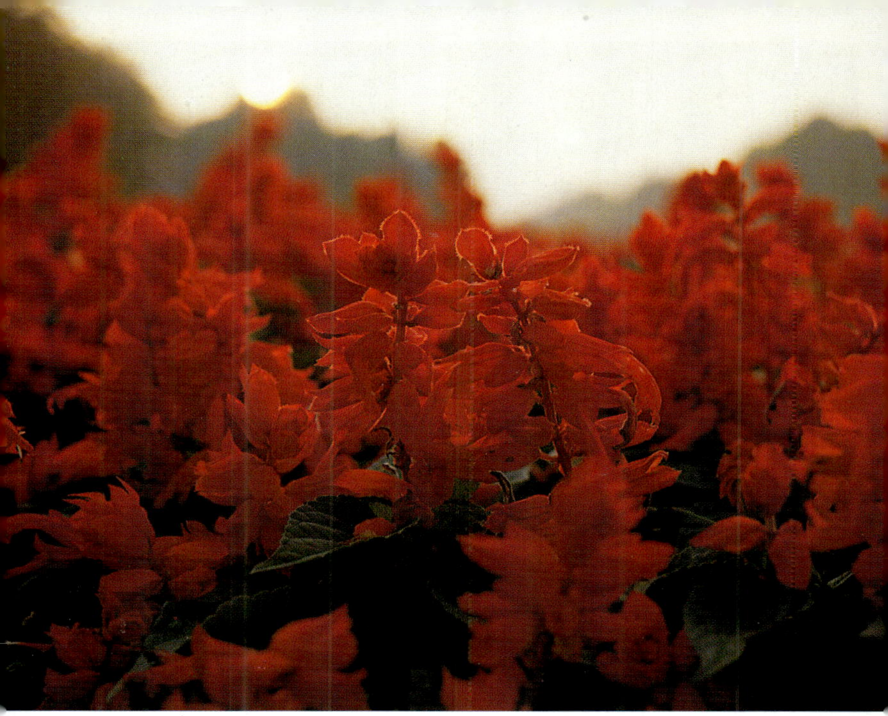

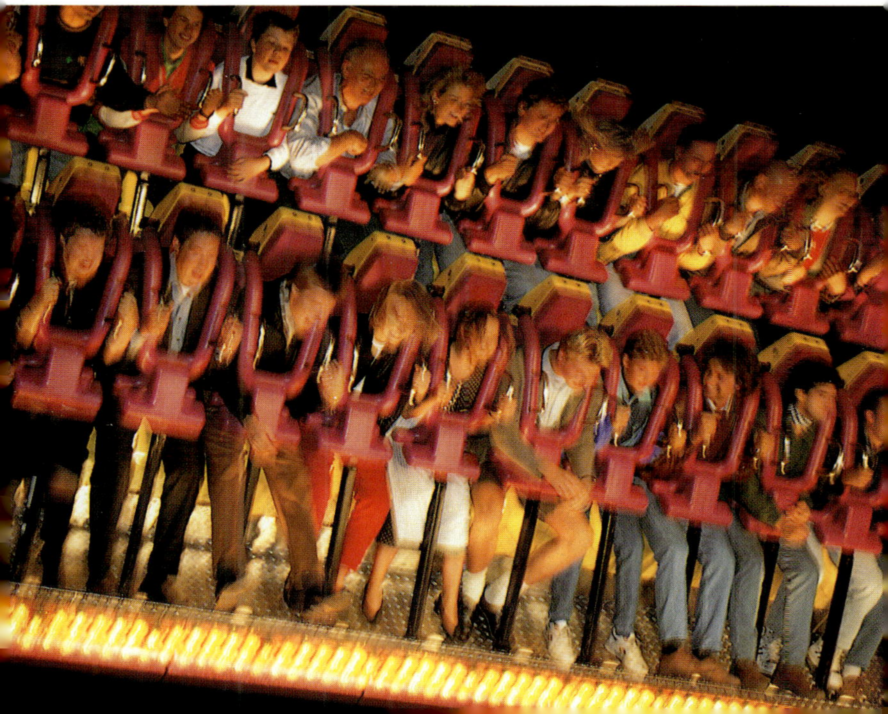

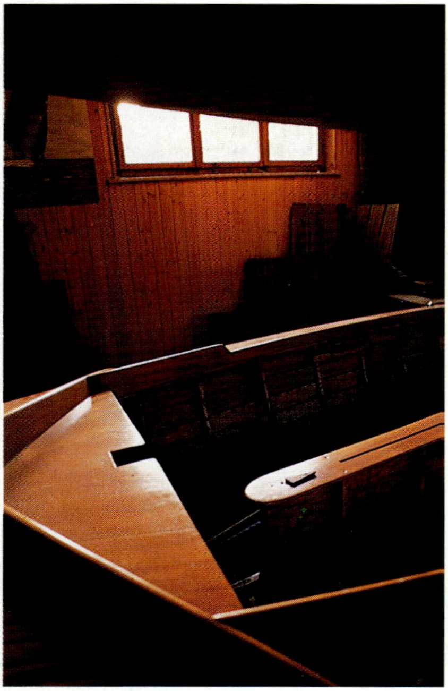
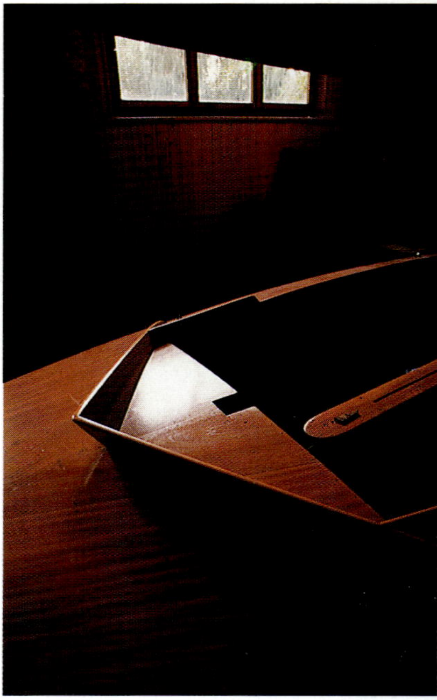
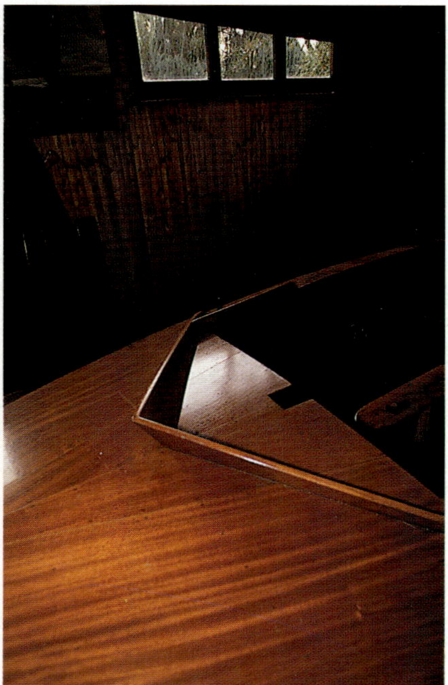
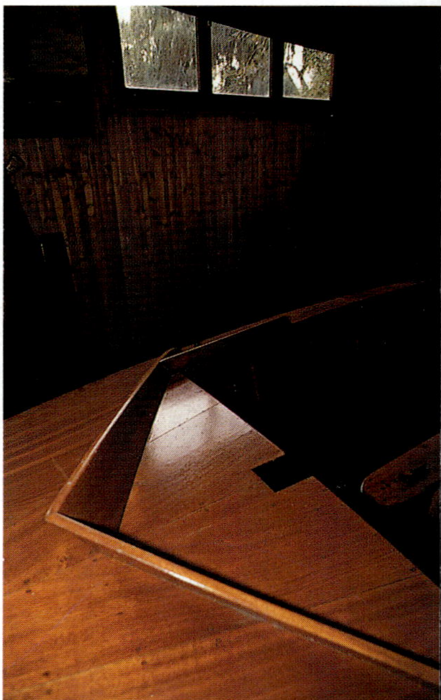

the form of specific number of revolutions, either forward or backward.

The motor's rotation is then reported back to the AF-IC. At the same time, the motor causes the focus system of the lens to turn via a mechanical hook-up and clutch When the lens focus setting is complete, the CPU checks the focus once more at the AF IC and, if confirmed, passes the information on to the viewfinder LCD where the "in-focus" symbol will appear. Ideally, all these operations from the double distance reading to the focusing of the lens and the viewfinder indication should take less than 1/10 second.

If the camera's CPU, after checking with the AF-IC, still detects an out-of-focus setting, the focusing process will be repeated by driving the lens focus from close-up to infinity. If again no focus setting is achieved, the CPU passes th s information on to the viewfinder display which will blink, indicating that a sharp picture is not possible.

The Definition of Sharpness

An image is said to be in focus if every point of an object at that same distance is reproduced as a sharp point on the film plane. If the distance is not properly set, then the points of an object do not have a sharp outline any longer and they melt together with other points surrounding them.

Out-of-focus images are the result of one of two things: distance set too close or distance set too far. If, for instance, an object is 5ft. away and the lens is set at 2ft., the light rays will form a sharp image in front of the film plane. To obtain sharpness, the lens should be turned towards the 5ft. setting, clockwise with Nikon lenses, until the light rays exactly form a sharp image on the film plane. If the lens is set to infinity instead of 5ft., the light rays of an object point will produce a sharp image behind the film plane. This means that the distance ring on the Nikon lens would have to be turned counter-clockwise.

Left top: With the N90/F90's program mode, and Matrix metered exposure correction, a good exposure was made using even without flash. In flash mode (the remaining three images), the light shining through the window is more balanced but the reflection of the flash on the subject is disturbing.

AF Light Paths:
With the help of a second mirror, the picture transmitted by the lens onto the semi-transparent main mirror is redirected to the CCD's condenser.

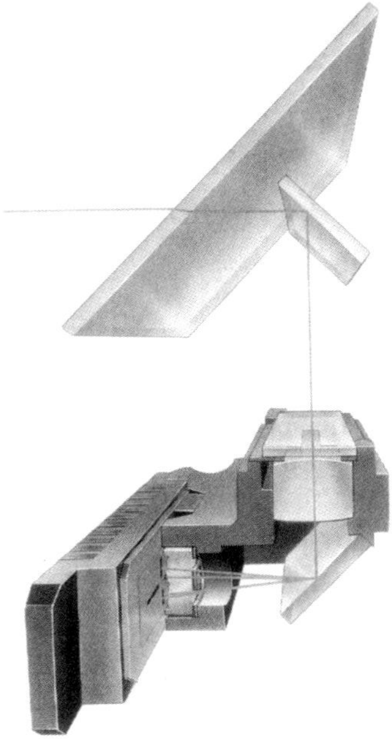

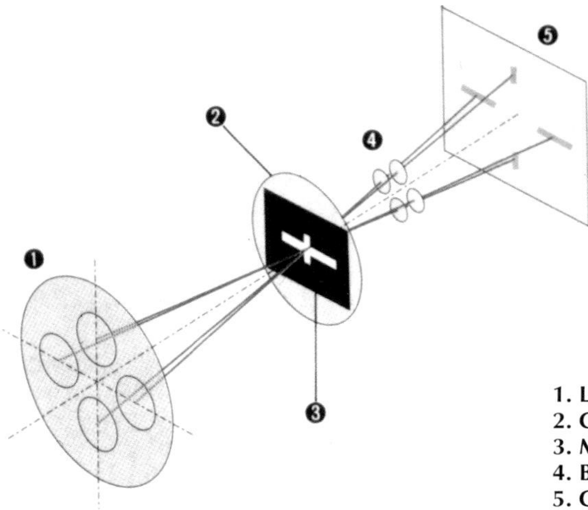

1. Lens
2. Condenser
3. Mask
4. Beam Splitters
5. CCD Sensors

Light Paths in the AF Sensor Module:
The image is divided into horizontal and vertical stripes by the mask. This image is transmitted onto sensors arranged in a cross-shaped pattern.

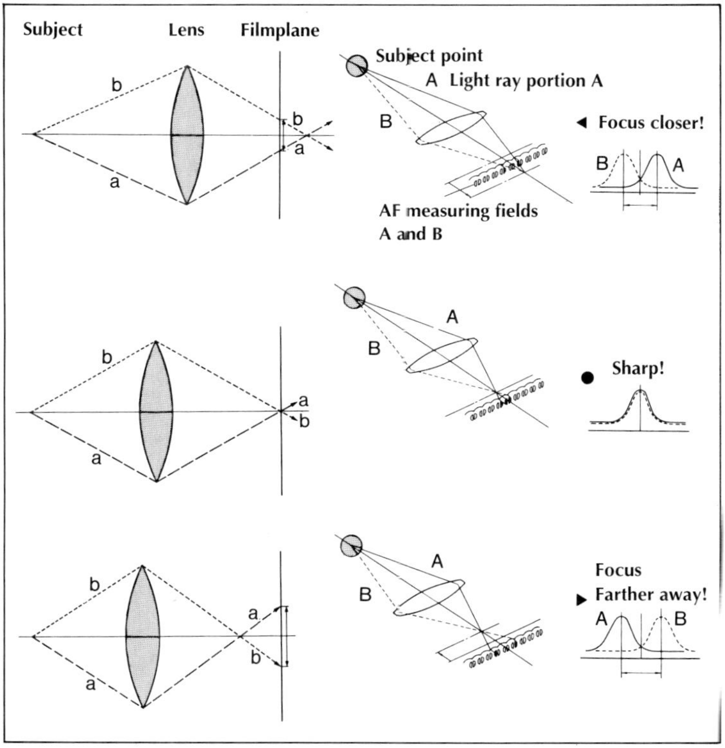

Principles of Phase Detection

The Task

It is therefore the task of the autofocus mechanism to read and evaluate the blurring of object points. First, the appropriate focusing movement has to be recognized, and second, the camera's CPU must calculate the necessary lens adjustment. To do this, the sensor group (CCD chip, plus evalutating IC), reads the expanding blurriness of object point caused by incorrect distance setting at the film plane. To be really accurate, the reading is not done on the film plane, but on a part of the picture that is redirected to the CCD via a secondary mirror instead.

Accurate Focusing

When the lens is focused at the proper distance, the light rays of the sharp object point are projected onto the AF sensor such that two neighboring reading fields receive practically all the light; field "A" from one half and field "B" the other half of the lens. The electronic focus IC evaluation is programmed in such a way that it will compare the curve of all "A" points with that of all "B" points. If the two curves overlap (the curves are in phase in electronic language) then the focus IC reports "picture in focus" to the central computer.

Out-of-Focus Images

When the lens is focused too close and the sharp image is in front of the film plane, the AF sensor will not only be illuminated by one set of blurred images, but by several. The result is that the curves of the "A" fields and "B" fields have separate peaks. The same thing happens if the lens is focused too far. Since the curve displacements for lens settings that are "too close" and "too far" are opposite of each other, the focus IC can determine what the focus correction should be, based on the phase shift between the two curves. These findings are transmitted to the camera's central computer. This data combined with other lens information is used to calculate the proper lens setting.

Exposure Control Modes

The N90/F90 has three automatic exposure modes. Between center-weighted, spot, and Matrix metering, there is an option for every situation. Additionally, if circumstances warrant, the N90/F90's exposure can be manually set.

Selection of Automatic Mode
While pressing the metering system button, turn the command dial.

❒ **Center-weighted metering -** In this mode, the brightness of a subject or scene is measured as follows: 75% from a large circle in the center and 25% from the rest of the picture. If the main subject is in the center, the result is normally a well exposed picture. If the main subject fills the whole frame and the exposure value is stored or manually selected, the result will be similar to spot metering results.

This method is very useful if you have enough time to measure the exposure of the subject manually. In comparison to spot metering and Matrix metering, I cannot see any advantages to this method. Thanks to the center-weighted exposure control, a photographer who uses several Nikon cameras interchangeably (e.g. F3 or FM-2), can use the same function on all cameras, without constantly having to rethink his or her actions.

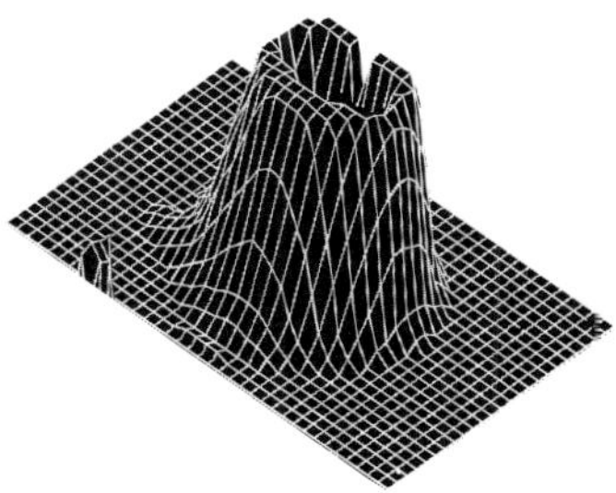

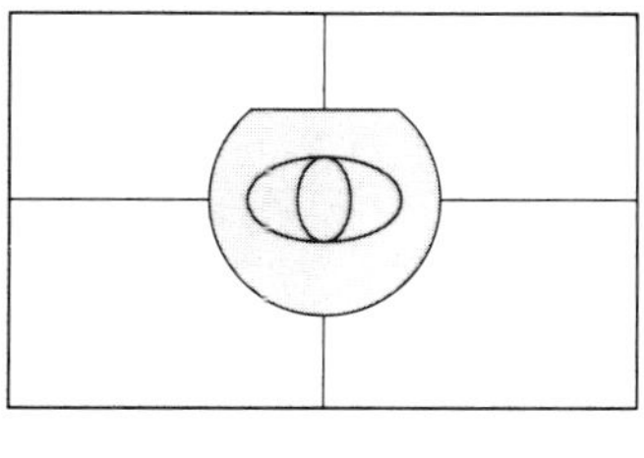

Integrated center-weighted metering with 75% of reading from the center of the image.

❐ **Spot metering -** Here, the subject's brightness is essentially measured in only the very center (1%) of the picture area. This permits extremely accurate measuring of subject details.

Since the degree of light reflection from the specific subject is very important, only experienced photographers will get good results. A lack of experience will lead to exposure errors when using the spot metering method. Even the professional should only use spot metering if the situation allows enough time for careful measurement.

Spot metering concentrates the reading on only 1% of the total picture area

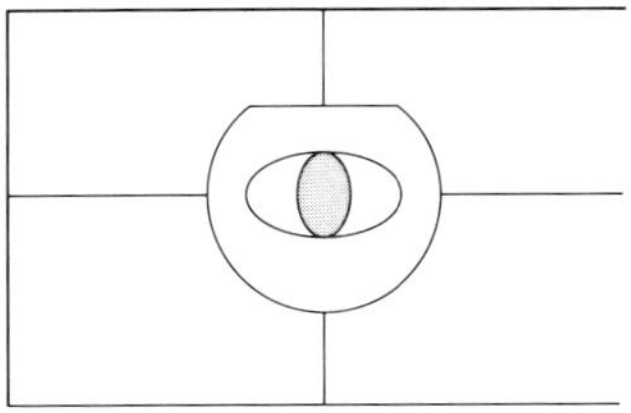

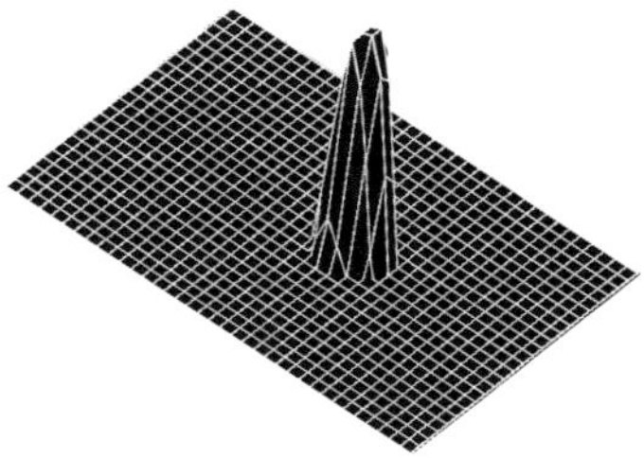

❐ **Matrix metering -** With Matrix metering, the brightness of a scene is measured in 8 separate areas of the picture. With the N90/F90 as well as with other contemporary Nikon cameras (N4004, N6006, N8008s, F4), the Matrix reading always works together with an automatic exposure correction (see below).

The 8-segment Matrix reading can be made with all AF Nikkor lenses in all exposure modes regardless of if you use multi-program mode, shutter priority mode, aperture priority mode, with or without (AE-L) auto-exposure lock or in manual mode.

❐ **Three-dimensional Matrix exposure -** This is only possible with the latest type D Nikkor lenses. Only these lenses report the subject distance to the N90/F90. When one of these lenses is attached, the camera automatically enters 3D mode. The N90/F90 uses all

The basis of the automatic Matrix metering system is an eight-segment reading. The reading is averaged over five segments and taken as exact in the other three.

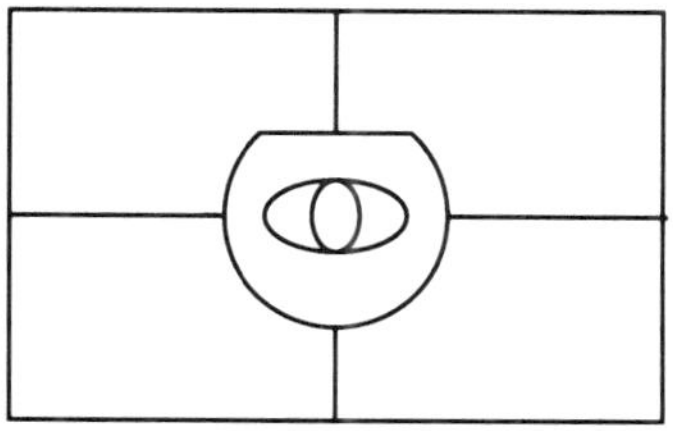

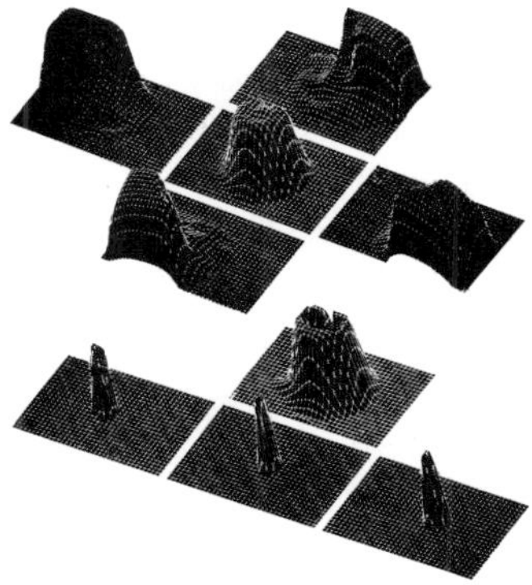

8 segments of the sensor but weights the information in relation to the distance setting. In addition, the N90/F90's 3D Matrix metering system recognizes main subjects that are off-center, and reads the focus in the center of the picture. If the center is out of focus, the N90/F90 recognizes that the composition has changed since focusing, and uses the outer segments to set the exposure.

❒ **Matrix operated exposure correction -** The camera's computer calculates an automatic exposure correction based on the total picture brightness and the brightness difference of the 8 segments (contrast). You do not, therefore, have to make any calculations yourself, nor do you have to make any adjustments on the camera.

The Dangers of Matrix

There are several situations which cause problems for the Matrix system.

❒ **Very small or very finely textured subjects -** If the main subject does not appear as a solid area in the frame, such as thin branches or a wire fence, the camera may not recognize it as a back-lit scene and will not make the appropriate exposure correction.

❒ **White on white** - The N90/F90's exposure correction calculation is obviously dependent on the film sensitivity and on how much of the picture area is white. It could happen that the Matrix control will expose a sun-lit snowscape properly, but it is more likely that the shot will be under-exposed (resulting in grey snow).

❒ **Black on black -** The N90/F90's proper exposure calculation obviously depends on how much of the picture area is black.

Scenes such as a chimney sweep in a coal cellar will result in an exposure error with the Matrix mode by overexposure (blacks will appear grey).

❐ **Back-lighting with slow film speeds under overcast skies:** Matrix metering may consider these conditions as a night scene and hence not calculate an increase in exposure time. An exposure in these conditions, therefore, may result in a well exposed sky but an under-exposed landscape.

Which Mode to Choose

There are some shooting situations where one cannot rely on the automatic exposure based on spot or center-weighted metering. In these specific cases, the photographer's experience is crucial. Even today's ambitious photographer does not like to switch to manual settings, nor does he always have the necessary correction values at hand. Exposure bracketing is also a relatively cumbersome solution and is not possible with many subjects. Matrix metering is therefore the ideal method if the photographer wants to concentrate on the subject without having to consider technical details. In hectic situations, this also applies to the professional. In approximately 80% of the cases, the results are good to very good.

Manual Exposure

If you want better results than you believe automatic Matrix can provide, you must switch to spot or center-weighted metering and manual ("M") exposure setting. In these cases, reading a grey card, the back of the hand, or direct reading of the main subject is necessary.

This picture of bizarre stone formations contains a large tonal range. The shot was taken by exposing for the middle-grey values. The film was then carefully processed so that an enlargement could be made on medium-grade enlarging paper to obtain bright whites, solid blacks, and good mid-range tonal graduation. ➪

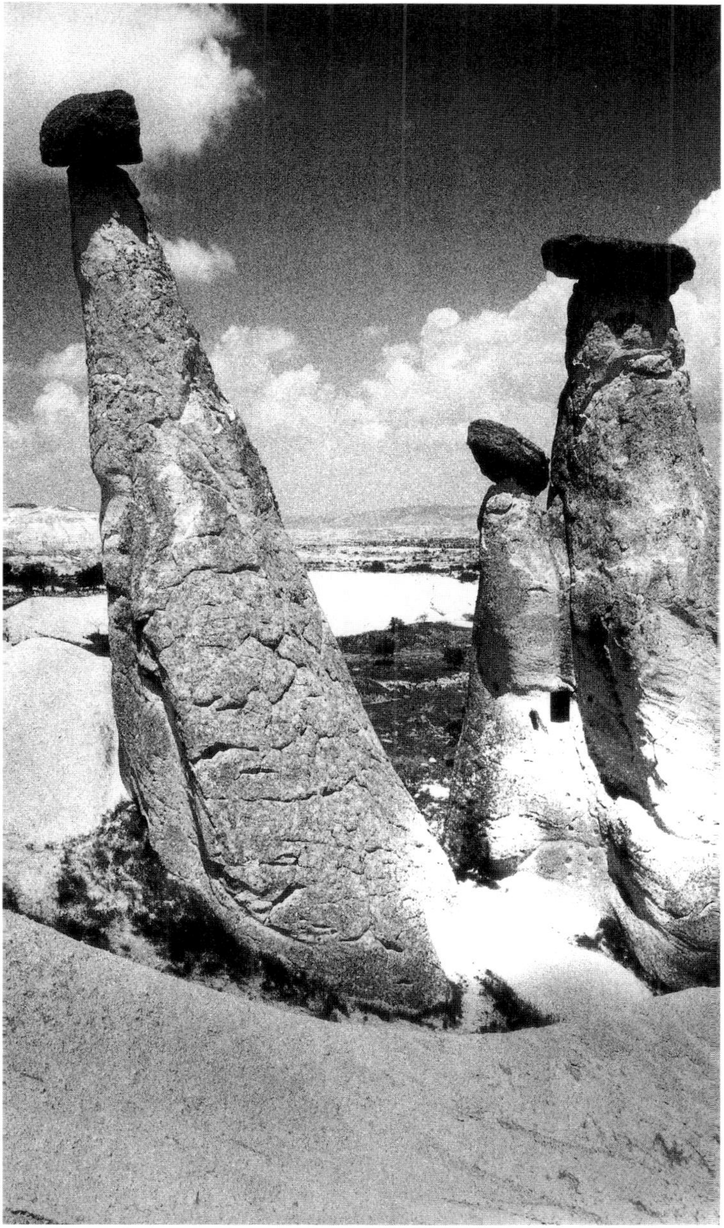

Manual Exposure Correction

By pressing down on the +/- button and turning the command dial, you can change the exposure manually from -5 EV to +5 EV in 1/3 stop increments.

It only makes sense to make individual manual exposure correction readings if the metering characteristics (spot or center-weighted) and the subject characteristics are well known. In Matrix metering mode, the manual exposure correction would add to the automatic correction a value that the photographer does not know, often resulting in an incorrect exposure.

❒ **Areas of application -** Manual exposure correction is particularly useful with all-black or all-white subjects. In combination with center-weighted or spot metering, the experienced photographer will be rewarded with outstanding results.

Remember that the selected film speed interacts with the metering and control of the N90/F90's electronics. With Matrix or center-weighted metering, using a film of ISO 100 and a lens with maximum aperture f/1.4, you have a range from EV 1 (corresponds to f/1.4 at 4 sec.) to EV 21 (f/22 at 1/4000 sec.). Unofficially, the range extends to EV 23 (f/32 at 1/8000 sec.) provided you use a lens that stops down that far. With spot metering, the control range with ISO 100 only extends from EV 3 to EV 21. With higher speed films, the exposure value numbers move towards lower EV values. With very slow films, ISO 6 for example, you can expose with higher exposure values.

Photography with Automatic Multi-Program

The principle of automated multi-program is simple: the camera automatically sets the shutter speed and the f-stop setting according to the film speed and the brightness of the subject. With the addition of autofocus, all that remains for the photographer to do is select the scene and frame the image in the viewfinder. Whether the aperture is small and the exposure time long, or the aperture large and the exposure time short, depends on the characteristics of the selected program mode, on the situation at hand, and on the lens being used. Whenever possible, the shutter speed is set slower for wide angle lenses and faster for telephoto lenses, provided that the speed is at least equal to the inverse of the focal length. The computer will only select an aperture that satisfies this condition. Blur due to camera shake is therefore avoided.

I personally find it inappropriate to call photographs taken in these modes "snapshots;" taking pictures without having to fiddle with f-stops and shutter speeds is important for capturing natural looking, unposed, and true-to-life photographs.

Procedure

To utilize this fully-automatic mode, set the lens to its minimum aperture (the highest number), and press the MODE button. While holding it down, turn the command dial until "P" is displayed in the LCD. Next, select the focusing mode (AF or manual), the size of the AF field, and the exposure mode. Now look through the viewfinder and activate the exposure reading and the autofocus system by lightly pressing down on the shutter button. In the center of the viewfinder display, you will find the symbol for the selected exposure method. To its right, you will see the computer's calculated shutter speed and the f-stop. With your subject in focus, you have nothing more to worry about and can release the shutter any time.

Possible Errors

If a conventional lens (without a built-in ROM chip) is used, the program symbol in the viewfinder will flash, and the camera will

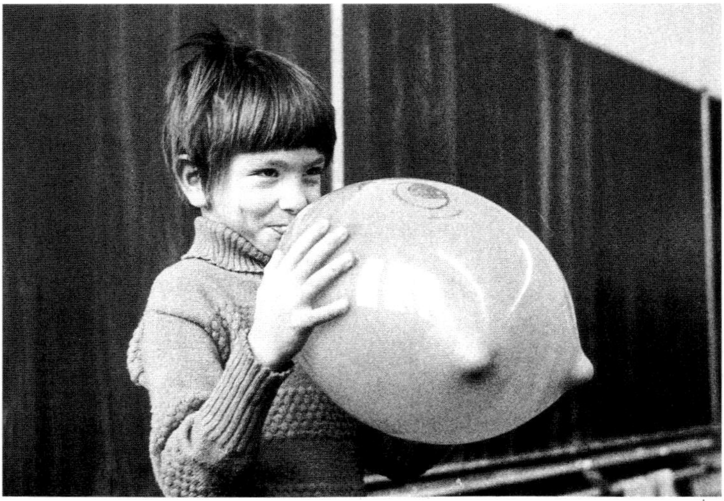

Pictures of children are usually stiff and posed. It is up to the photographer to catch the moment when the child is acting "normally," even while being watched.

automatically select a middle range shutter speed so that your picture will be correctly exposed. Please note that no f-stop value is shown in the viewfinder when non-AF lenses are used. There are a variety of other indicators that will appear in the LCD if there is a problem.

❐ **"EE" -** You forgot to set the lens to its smallest f-stop.

❐ **"HI" -** Your scene is so bright that the exposure range of the N90/F90 is exceeded, and you will have an over-exposed frame. With color negative or black and white film there is no harm in over-exposing a little bit. With slides, you should use a neutral density filter.

❐ **"LO" -** Danger of under-exposure is indicated. You probably will have to use flash.

❐ **Audible beep -** Danger of blurring due to camera movement. The shutter speed calculated by the camera's computer is slower than the inverse of the focal length used. You should shift the program to a faster speed, rest the camera on a solid surface, or better still, use a tripod.

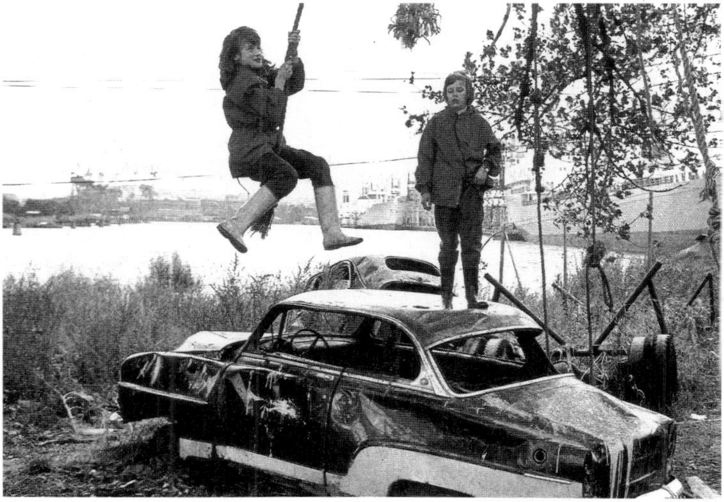

Again, the photographer is responsible for catching the spontaneous actions of children at play.

Applications

For the professional, this mode is useful when he or she wants to concentrate only on the subject matter. In addition, anyone who does not like to think in technical terms is also greatly assisted by this automation.

Recommended Lenses

The most useful lenses range from 28mm to 135mm. Considerably shorter or longer focal lengths are usually used for special subjects or scenes and require special settings for shutter speed and aperture.

Recommended Films

Medium film speeds are recommended. The most commonly used transparency film speed is ISO 100 and for color negatives, ISO 200. Multi-program mode is not generally used for subjects that require extremely slow or fast films.

Manual Program-Shift

The automatically selected exposure setting found by the multi-program mode can be manually changed. Using the command dial, you can adjust the aperture and shutter speed while maintaining the same exposure value. You can therefore stay in multi-mode while doing the equivalent of changing to shutter or aperture priority. If the shutter speed is too long or too short for your subject, or if the aperture is too large or small, simply shift to the desired speed or f-stop.

❒ **Procedure** - After lightly depressing the shutter release, the N90/F90's automatic exposure reading system is activated. The calculated exposure is displayed in the viewfinder: shutter speed and f-stop appear in the center of the LCD. This f-stop/speed combination can now be altered by simply turning the command dial. The amount of light reaching the film remains constant, but shutter speed and f-stop change inversely in full stops. If, for example, the LCD showed f/8 at 1/250, and you turn the command dial counter-clockwise, you get f/5.6 at 1/500. If you keep turning, you will find a reading of f/4 at 1/1000. Turning clockwise, f/8 at 1/250 becomes f/11 at 1/125 etc. When the picture is taken, the selected "program-shift" is erased, and the original program is reinstated.

Photography with Subject Optimized Vari-Programs

This type of automation makes its Nikon debut on the N90/F90. By selecting one of seven preset programs, the photographer has at his or her fingertips the right tools for a very specific job. In other words, the photographer need not worry about setting any situation-specific parameters. It is done automatically.

❒ **Procedure** - While pressing the "PS" button (to the left of the viewfinder), turn the command dial to one of the seven programs.

"Po" - Portrait Program

This mode sets the camera to produce an in-focus subject with a slightly blurred background.

❒ **Recommended lens and exposure method** - Autofocus lenses from 80mm to about 200mm with a maximum aperture of f/2.8 combined with Matrix metering is recommended. The "Po"

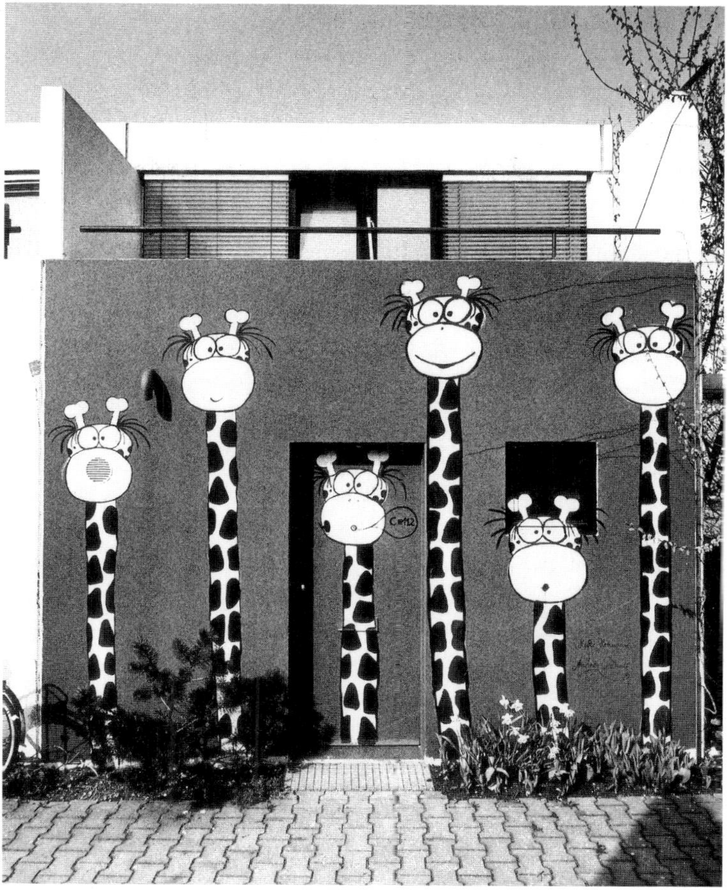

Many photographers enjoy documenting everyday "street" art.

program is not very useful with slow lenses, and requires fast lenses such as the Nikkor 85mm f/1.8.

❐ **Performance test** - During my tests, the "portrait program" always used an aperture of f/2.8 or slightly higher, regardless of the film speed (ISO 100 to 400) or the subject brightness.

❐ **Verdict** - In my opinion, the "portrait program" takes the easy way out. After all, you do not always need the largest possible aperture with various camera/subject and subject/background distances. And while this program prevents complete disasters, in some cases, a pro could be up to one f-stop more accurate.

"rE" - Portrait with Flash and Pre-flash

In this mode, the desired effect is the same as above, but it adds a red-eye prevention feature.

❐ **Recommended lens and exposure method -** Same as above. Please note, however, that red-eye prevention is possible only when using the SB-25.

❐ **Performance test -** Because the SB-25's reflector is situated relatively high above the lens axis and the light quality is relatively soft, you will rarely have a red-eye problem, even without this mode. On the plus side, though, pre-flash does help eliminate squinting eyes and more unnatural facial expressions.

❐ **Verdict -** Marginally useful.

"SL" - Silhouette Program

The purpose of this mode is to facilitate the difficult task of creating attractive silhouettes.

❐ **Recommended lens and exposure method -** Any mid-range lens will work fine in this mode. As far as exposure goes, the background has to be at least two f-stops brighter than the subject; the camera will take care of this for you, but do not use a flash. The silhouette program permits long exposure times which, in turn, could result in blurs due to camera shake. If possible, use a tripod.

❐ **Performance test -** In my test, the silhouette program did indeed select an exposure of two to three exposure steps slower than the bright background would have required. A pro would have to take meter readings with great effort to obtain the same or better picture.

❐ **Verdict -** Very useful.

"HF" - Hyper Focal Program

In order to obtain the maximum depth of field with wide angle or normal focal length lenses, one should use a small aperture opening (high f-stop number). The danger is blurring due to camera shake or object movement, both caused by small apertures.

❐ **Recommended lens and exposure method -** Autofocus lenses from 50mm down to 20mm using Matrix metering. Since the "HF" program may select longer exposure speed that the inverse of the focal length, a tripod must be used in certain instances.

❒ **Performance test** - In my tests, the "hyper focal" program always selected f/11 as long as the film speed (ISO 100 to 400) and lens speed permitted.

I frequently take landscape pictures with the 20mm where I occasionally need an aperture of f/16 or f/22 to get the near foreground up to infinity in focus. It is logical that with f/11 one has relatively good depth of field, but not as good as with f/22.

❒ **Verdict** - Not very useful.

"LA" - Landscape Program

This mode sets the camera to a distant focal setting and a small aperture, both necessary for landscape photography.

❒ **Recommended lens and exposure method** - AF lenses from 20mm and Matrix metering. You may sometimes have to use a tripod since slow shutter speeds are often chosen. Nikon's advice to use faster film is, in my opinion, too generalized. The detail breakup is critical, particularly in landscape pictures. This end is better acheived with ISO 100 than ISO 400.

❒ **Performance test** - In my tests, the landscape program selected apertures from f/5.6 to f/16, whenever focal length, lens speed and brightness permitted. This is equivalent to what an experienced photographer would have chosen.

It is important to remember that landscapes taken with wide-angle lenses frequently result in large sky areas, and even with Matrix reading this often leads to under-exposed pictures. Setting the exposure manually by reading the subject without the sky is far better.

❒ **Verdict** - Conditionally useful, but does not satisfy professional demand in critical situations.

"SP" - Sport program

This program is designed to select the relatively short shutter speeds required when using long focal length lenses to prevent motion blur or movement by the photographer. If the exposure speeds are too short, however, any movement is unnaturally frozen.

❒ **Recommended lens and exposure method** - The focal length of the lens should be between 80 and 300mm and the speed, if

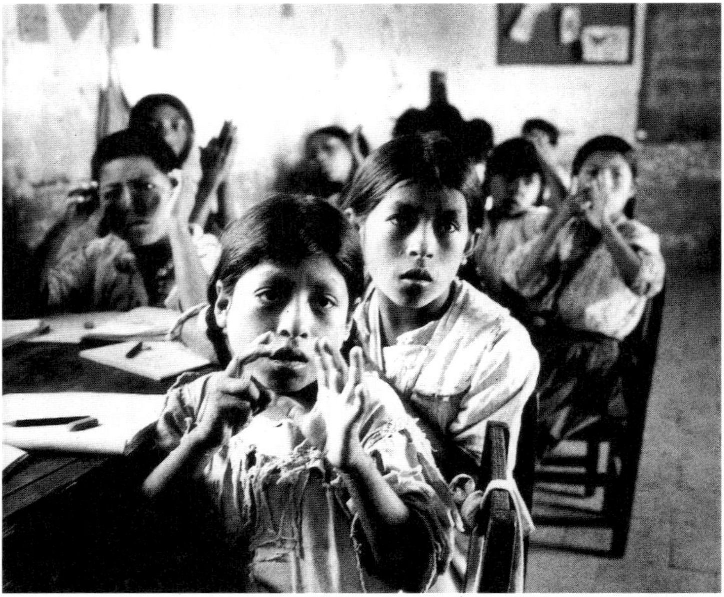

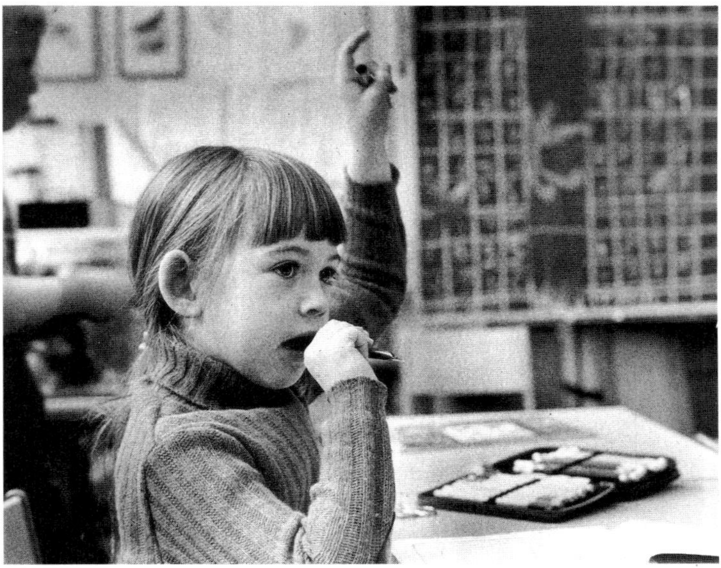

possible, f/2.8. According to my tests, you will need ISO 400 film. Even higher film sensitivities are needed to compensate for low light conditions. In most cases, it is recommended to use AF mode "C" with film transport "C" to have the camera set for continuous focusing. Matrix metering is once again your best bet.

❐ **Performance test -** During my tests, the "sport program" selected speeds of 1/250 or 1/500 whenever it was possible with existing subject brightness, film speed, and lens speed.

Unfortunately, the camera cannot judge the difference between frozen action and no action at all.

❐ **Verdict -** Partially useful.

"CU" - Close-up Program

This program sets the camera for close-up photography. While it is certainly not macro, this program does provide some good close-up results.

❐ **Recommended lens and exposure method -** Contrary to the N90/F90 instruction manual, normal focal length lenses up to mid-telephoto lenses can be used (real telephoto lenses are not useful in macro photography). The close-up program allows slower shutter speeds that could result in blurred images. In these cases, use a tripod.

❐ **Performance test -** In my tests, the close-up program always selected f/4 with lenses under 28mm and f/5.6 with 28mm and higher, with the resulting magnification between 1:10 and 1:6. In real close-up photography (from about 1:4) or even macro photography (from 1:2), this program is completely useless because the depth of field gets smaller as the magnification ratio increases, making it necessary to use smaller apertures. As every professional knows, the important thing here is to compromise between maximum depth of field and minimum refraction (optimal f-stop).

❐ **Verdict -** Use with caution!

⇦ **If the theme is school, it must be made absolutely clear to the observer whether the children are in Bolivia or in Germany.**

The Final Word on Vari-Programs

Since the N90/F90 can be programmed from the outside via the Data-Link, a distinct improvement of the vari-programs with a new chip would not be impossible. Programs to calculate focal length, distance selection, and magnification would be desirable, especially for portrait and macro photography. Every professional would surely welcome a true depth of field program that would take the close and far focus points in consideration as well as the focal length and distance.

Program Automatics

Program automatics calculate the correct exposure value to achieve proper exposure for the existing subject brightness and the film speed used. They are what make the N90/F90's level of automation possible. The light values are automatically converted into a correct combination of shutter speed and aperture according to a program curve. In other words, the program automatic selects the correct speed/f-stop combination depending on the selected mode, either multi-program or one of the subject modes, from a multitude of such combinations.

Top: Here you see that the N90/F90's Matrix metering system can, in fact, fail.
Bottom: Using spot metering on the light grey cabin roof resulted in an automatic 3 stop improvement in exposure.

Page 88:
Top and Center: Both center-weighted and Matrix metering of this predominantly white subject resulted in a greyish picture. The non-white areas of the total image were not sufficient enough to modify the Matrix reading.
Bottom: Only a spot reading on the white sail with an additional manual exposure correction of +2 f/stops resulted in correct density.

Page 89:
Top: Matrix metering usually corrects any exposure discrepancies. Automatic exposure resulted in the correct mood for a sunset.
Bottom: Since the main subject's magnification is not too great, about 1:5, the depth of field provided by the close-up program (f/5.6) is sufficient. This aperture would not be sufficient with larger magnification ratios.

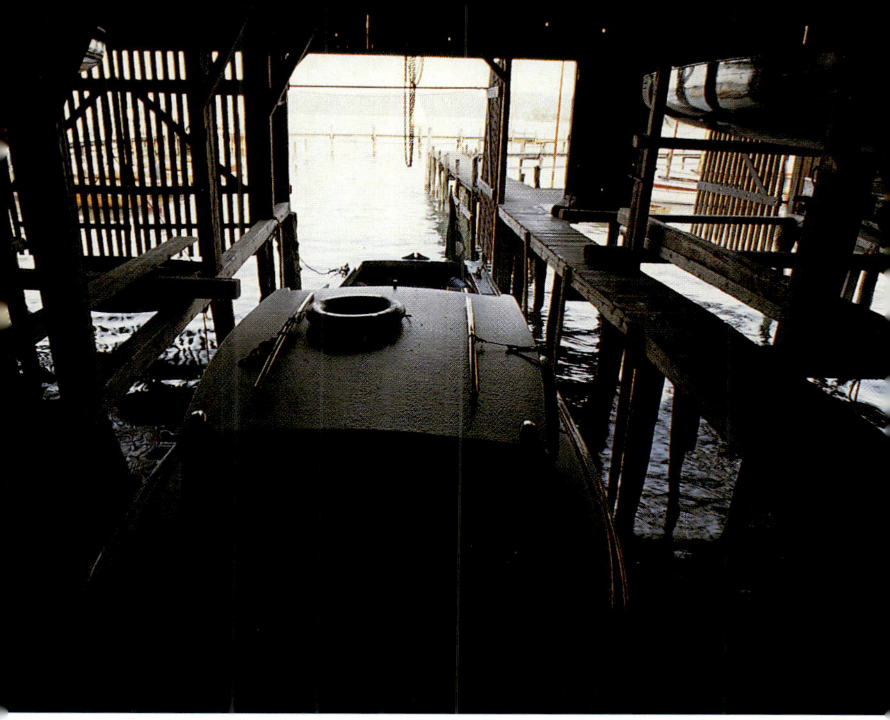

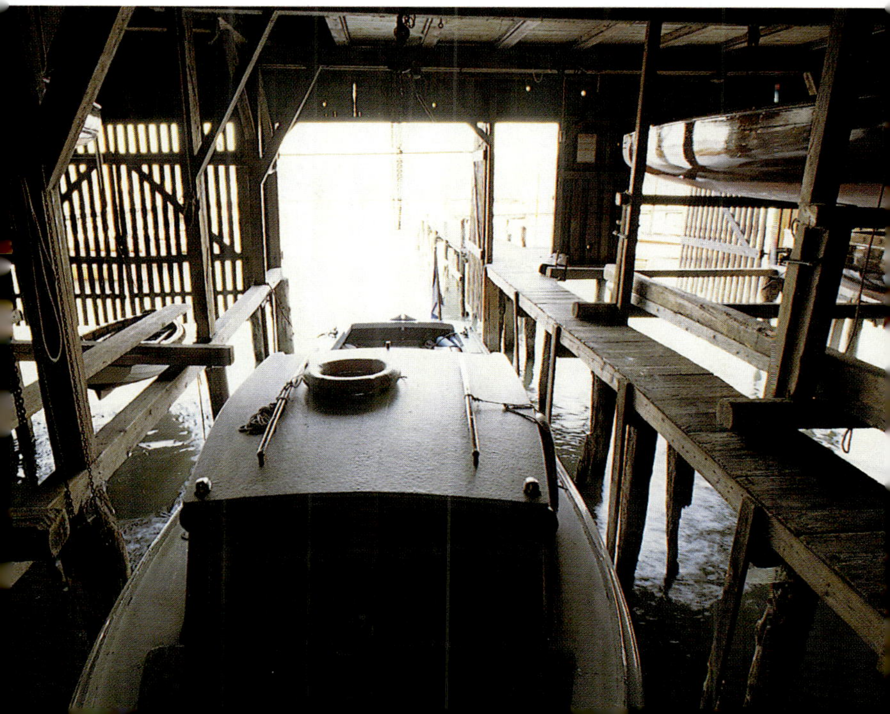

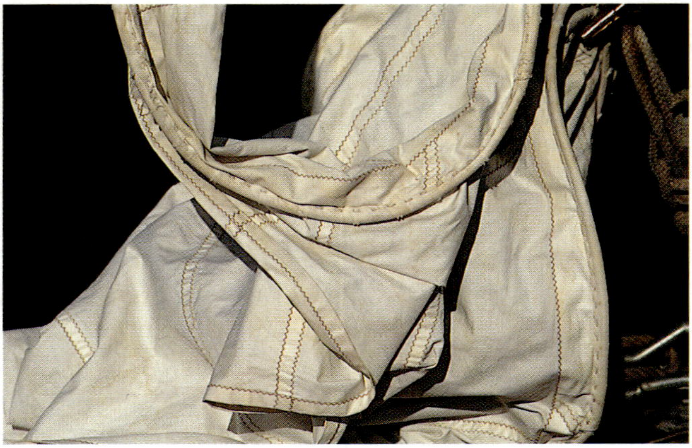

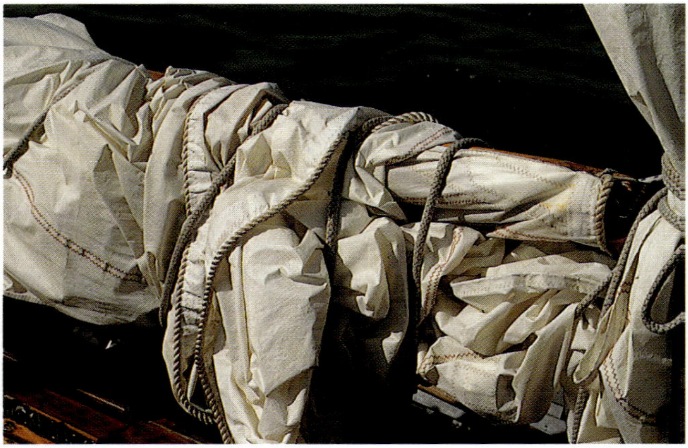

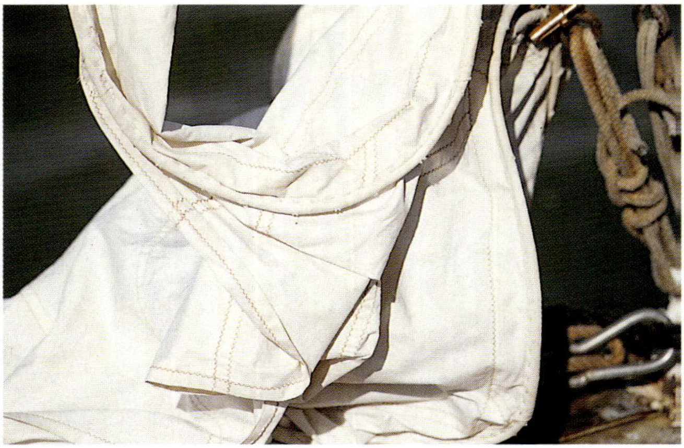

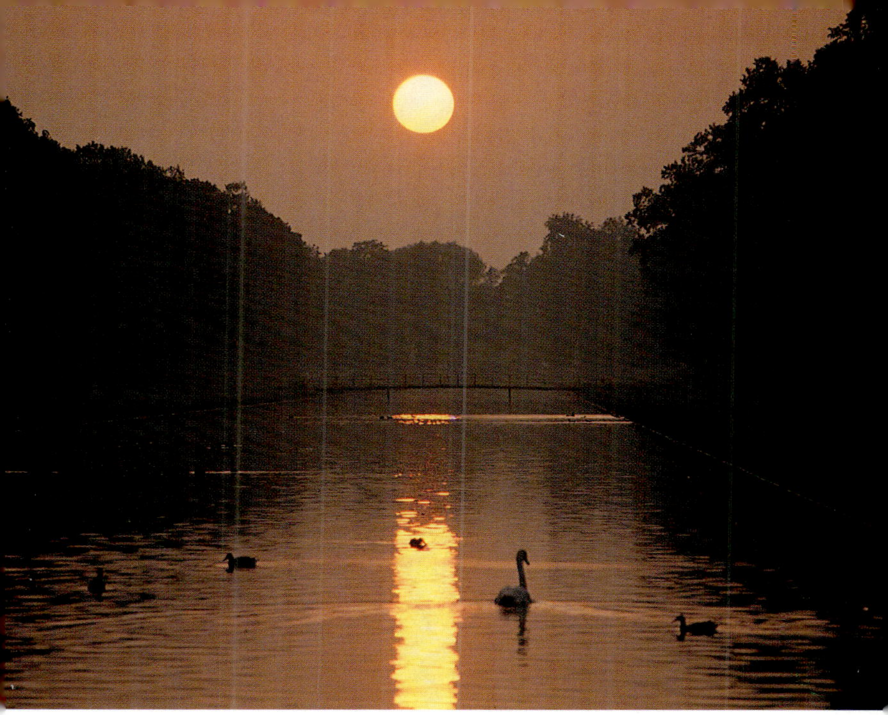

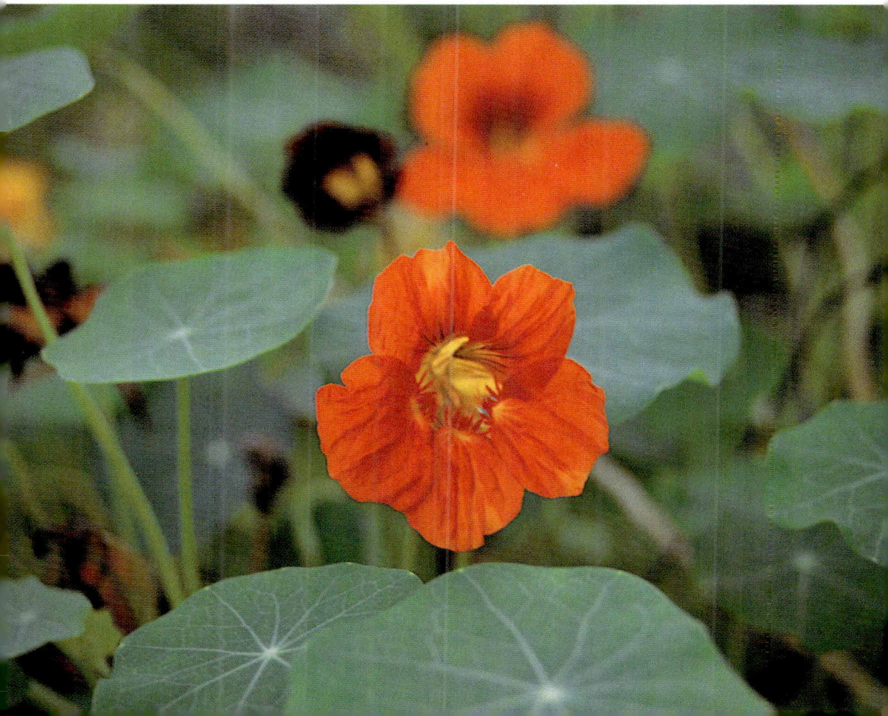

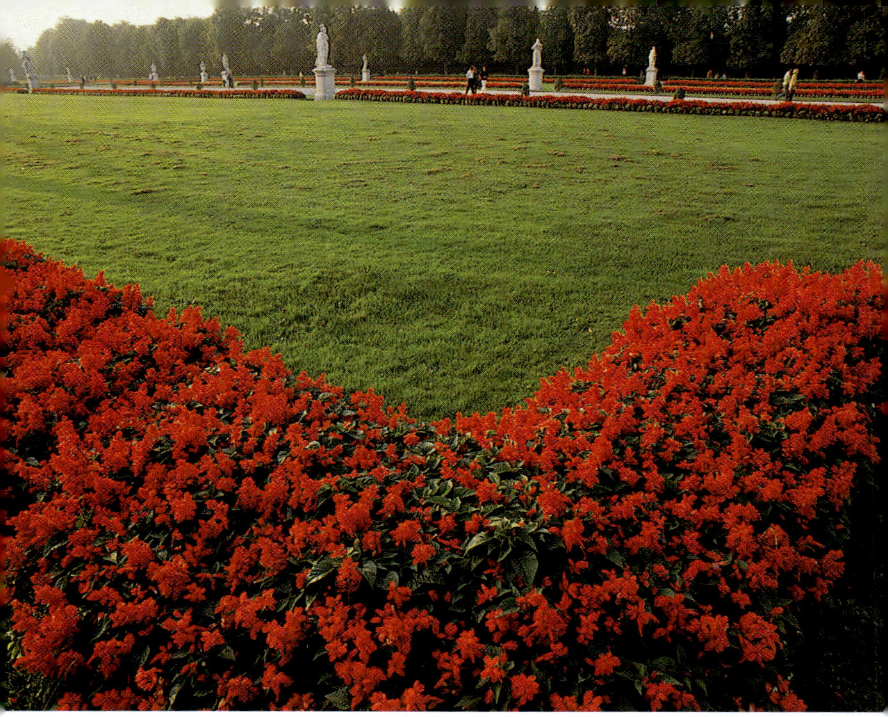

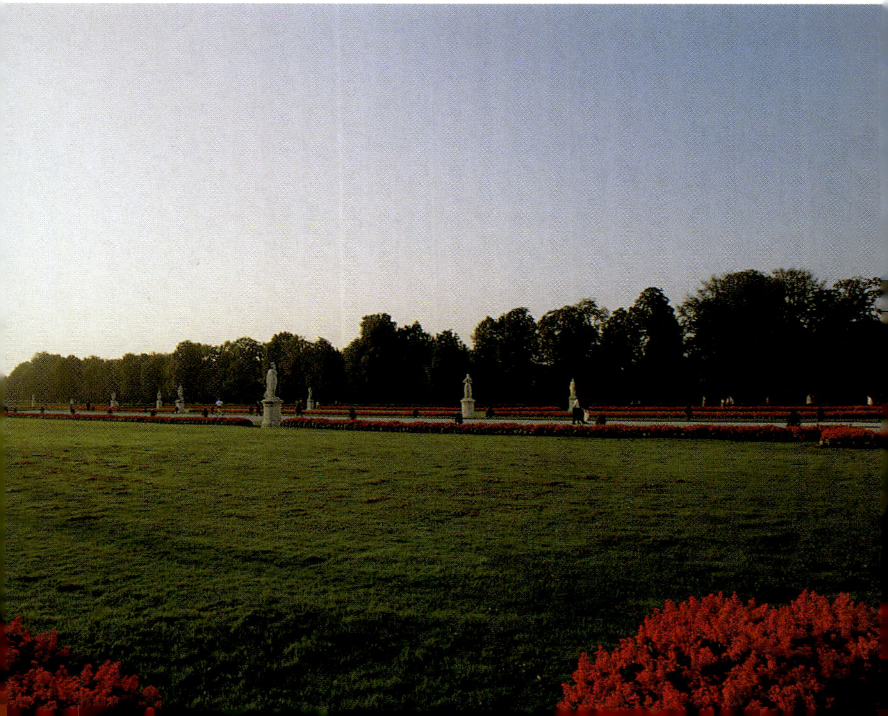

The Diagrams

The following exposure value/aperture/speed diagrams illustrate the N90/F90's program curves. In other words, these curves indicate at which light value the program automatic will expose with which aperture/speed combination. One exposure value "EV" is nothing more than a numerical measurement of the exposure. The EV number of a specific exposure value always represents a multiple of equally effective aperture/speed combinations. Equally effective means that all these combinations have the same result as far as the exposure is concerned. You will find more information regarding exposure, aperture, shutter speed and exposure value in the chapter "The Basics of Exposure."

Multi-program Curve

The main attraction of the multi-program mode is its ability to adapt the program curve to the speed and focal length of the lens being used. This is also ideal with zoom lenses where the focal length covers a large range from wide angle to telephoto and where the speed, in many cases, changes with the focal length used. Here are some practical examples. Let's assume that the scene is lit by a 60W bulb.

❒ **Zoom lens set at 28mm f/3.5 -** With ISO 100 film, this scene equals about EV 2. At EV 2, the multi-program automatic will calculate f/2.8 or f/4 with an exposure time of approximately 3 seconds. If, however, the camera reads a light value of EV 12, (a correct exposure under dense clouds with ISO 100), the automatic program would calculate f/8 at 1/60 second. With EV 20 (a picture in noon sunshine with blue sky at ISO 100), a setting of f/22 at 1/2000 would be calculated and adjusted.

Top: The landscape program usually results in well-exposed pictures as far as the automatic selection of aperture is concerned.

Bottom: Whenever the sky forms a large portion of the picture, however, the Matrix-controlled exposure usually fails. This also happens with other automatic exposure modes.

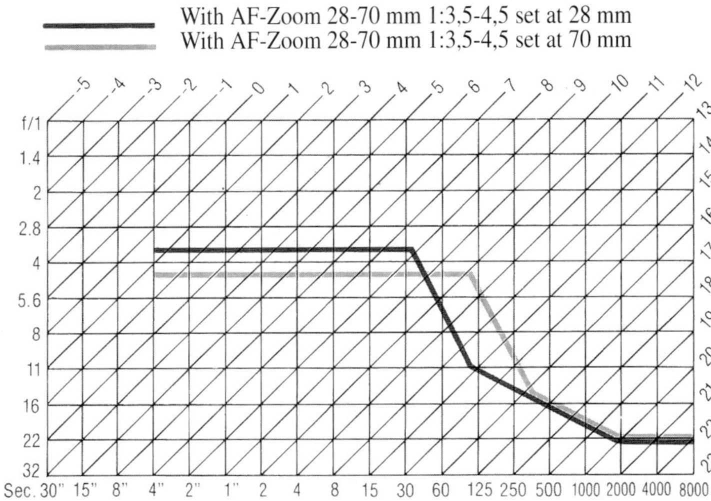

Multi-Program-Curve.

❒ **Zoom lens set at 70mm f/4.5 -** In this case the program curve starts at EV 2 due to the lower f-stop (4.5) and the exposure would be f/4 or f/5.6 at 3 seconds. At EV 12, the curve shows that the aperture will be close to f/5.6 at first, but the exposure at 1/125 second is shorter than the wide angle shot. This moderate stopping down with shorter shutter speeds continues to EV 16, where the curves for both focal lengths combine again.

Vari-program Curves

These curves are modified versions of those found for shutter or aperture priority modes, depending on the program. The difference is that the photographer does not set the f-stop or the shutter speed; the program takes care of it.

Understanding the Curves

In order to understand these curves, you should keep in mind which conditions remain constant and which vary during any given shot. Nikon makes the confusing statement that "at ISO 100,

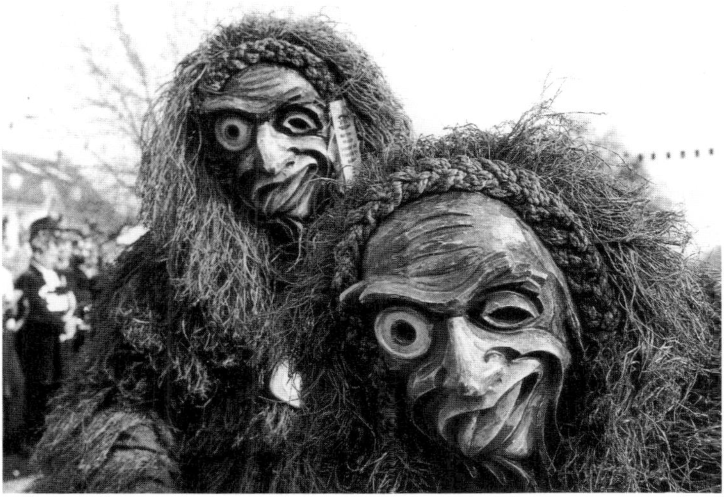

In the uproar of a carnival in Schwaben, the same rules apply as for sport and action.

the track of the curve does not depend on the film speed." What is really variable is the subject brightness and the film speed. If you already use a film of a specific speed in the camera, the light value with the program automatically uses to set shutter speed and f-stop depends only on the subject brightness. If, however, the subject brightness is given and you are still deciding which film to use, simply slide along the curve to arrive at larger f-stops and shorter shutter speeds when selecting films with higher ISO numbers.

Limits of the Program Curves

If we look at the multi-program curve, we notice that from EV 11 (at f/4.5) towards lower values, the program only changes shutter speeds depending on lens speed and focal length. In other words, the aperture remains wide open and the exposure correction takes place only by lengthening the shutter speed (depending on film speed, up to 30 seconds). At extremely high light values of EV 20 (f/22 at 1/2000) to EV 22, the curve shows constant aperture and changes shutter speed to 1/8000 second. With lenses that have

Manual Photography: Shutter Priority

When using the N90/F90's shutter priority (shutter preferred) mode, the photographer selects a specific shutter speed and the camera automatically selects the appropriate aperture, depending on the subject brightness and the film speed. You always use the shutter preferred mode when a specific shutter speed is required and the aperture is of secondary importance. The shutter preferred mode is especially recommended when photographing moving objects or with long focal length telephoto lenses due to the danger of camera shake.

Procedure

After inserting the film, set the aperture ring on the lens to the highest number, and then select the "S" mode using the MODE button and the command dial. Select the exposure mode, the AF mode and the AF field size. Once you have considered the conditions of the situation, select the appropriate shutter speed. Aim at the subject, slightly depress the trigger, and the shutter speed together with the camera-selected aperture will appear in the viewfinder and on the LCD panel. If you want to use a different shutter speed, simply turn the command dial. With the newly selected speed, the camera will indicate a newly calculated aperture.

Compatible Lenses

Only lenses with built-in ROM chips such as AF Nikkors and AI-P Nikkors can be used. Lenses without electrical contacts, with fixed apertures, or those where no aperture value transmission is possible cannot be used with shutter priority mode.

❐ **Using conventional lenses -** If you try to use a conventional lens in the shutter priority mode, the N90/F90 sets off a warning signal by flashing the shutter preferred symbol. The camera also switches automatically to aperture preferred mode with center weighted metering. Again, an improperly exposed photograph is avoided.

With non-AF lenses, you will not see any f-stop reading in the viewfinder display in any exposure mode, and it is recommended that you set the camera to aperture preferred mode and center-weighted metering.

Recommendations

❐ **Areas of application -** If you want to deliberately control the motion of a subject, the shutter preferred mode is the best choice. It is logical that longer exposure times and moving objects do not agree with each other. A race car that shows up as a colorful streak in the picture may win the race but not a photo contest.

On the other hand, it is also not always correct to "freeze" all movement. A gymnast that appears as a frozen pillar may be interesting to the coach, but the picture will not look realistic to most observers. The art of correctly exposing moving objects, therefore, consists of selecting a shutter speed that is not so slow that movements are badly blurred, and not so fast that movement is no longer visible. If you tried this before and were not very happy with the results, I can offer you some consolation: even famous sport photographers throw out 95% of their pictures in search of that one-in-a-million shot.

If, when shooting with long exposure times, you use a tripod or rest the camera on something, you should always use the self-timer or a remote triggering cord to prevent wiggling the unit during shutter release. And don't forget to close the built-in eyepiece shutter! When the eye is not at the ocular, light comes into the viewfinder and results in erroneous metering.

❐ **Appropriate lenses -** The most suitable lenses are telephoto lenses with focal lengths of about 80mm to 500mm. Considerably shorter or longer focal lengths are generally only used for specific subjects when exact selection of shutter speeds or apertures is necessary.

❐ **Appropriate films -** I recommend films with speeds of ISO 400 upwards. For specific subjects that require noticeably slower film speeds, one would not use the shutter preferred mode.

Error Warnings

Wrong exposures are actually impossible because you are immediately alerted to any problems and one glance at the viewfinder display will give you all necessary information. A variety of symbols are used to relay warning information.

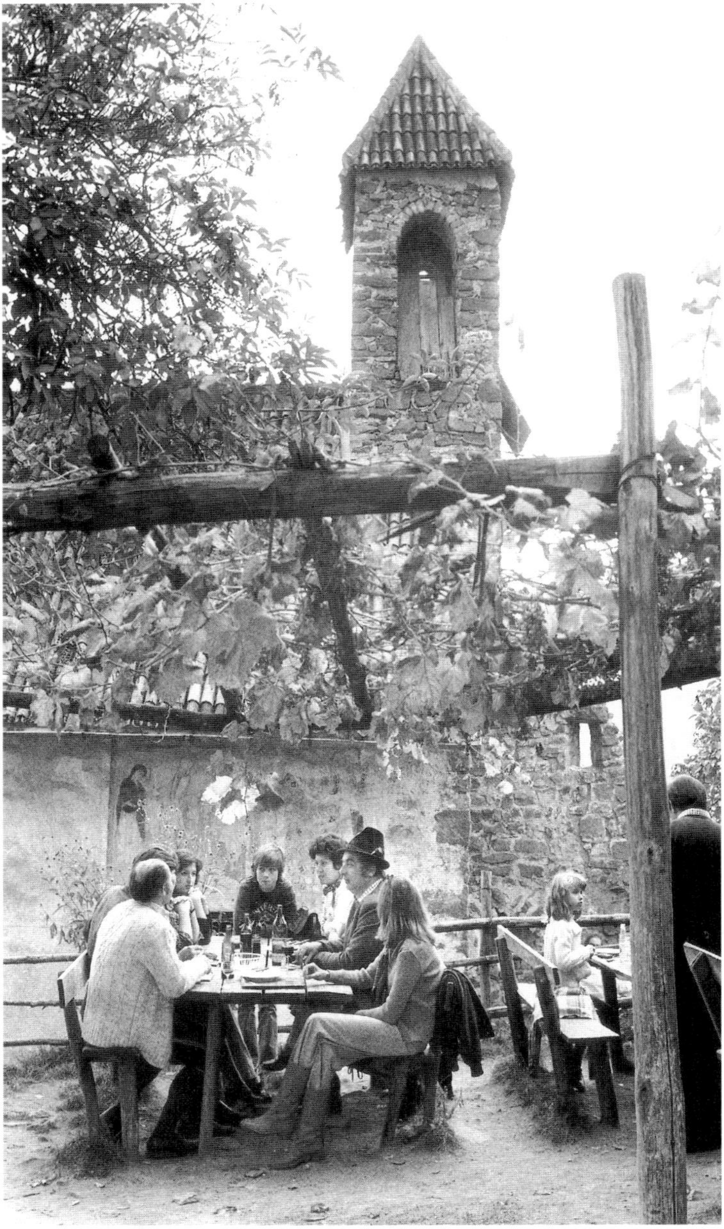

❐ **"EE"** - If this appears in the viewfinder instead of the f-stop value, you forgot to set the aperture ring on the lens to the smallest opening (highest number).

❐ **"HI"** - This indicates that the subject is so bright that it is beyond the control range of the N90/F90 and there is danger of overexposure. If you use color negative or black and white film, you can sometimes overexpose a little, but with slide film you should use a neutral density filter.

❐ **"LO"** - Here you are warned that there is not enough light, and an under-exposed photography result could occur. In these cases, you should use a flash.

Understanding Shutter Priority

After you pre-select the exposure time and touch the shutter button, the camera's computer calculates the appropriate aperture. To calculate the aperture, the computer evaluates the subject illumination, the film speed, the set exposure time and the aperture range of the current lens. The computer receives the information with respect to the smallest and largest possible apertures via the appropriate contacts from the lens' ROM. As soon as the shutter release is completely depressed, the computer sets the calculated aperture on the lens using a very fast motor and the spring-loaded aperture lever. After the mirror flips out of the way and the shutter opens, the film is exposed for the selected amount of time.

In this idyllic scene under the grape vines, the surroundings are just as important as the main subject. Careful selection of focus distance and aperture are critical to produce necessary depth of field.

Manual Photography: Aperture Priority

The basic principle of aperture priority (aperture preferred) mode is that the camera automatically selects a shutter speed to correspond to a user-selected aperture.

Procedure

While pressing the MODE button, turn the command dial until "A" appears in the LCD. Select the AF mode and field size, frame your subject, and select an appropriate f-stop on the aperture ring. Lightly press the shutter button and the selected aperture appears on the viewfinder LCD row and on the central LCD panel together with the camera's calculated exposure time. If you want to change the aperture, simply turn the lens' aperture ring and the new exposure time will appear. As long as no warning appears on the viewfinder display, you are guaranteed a correct exposure and can concentrate on aesthetics.

Compatible Lenses

Should you use a traditional, non-AF lens with mechanical aperture transmission (that is, without a ROM chip), the camera will display "-" instead of an aperture value. This means that the N90/F90 can no longer use Matrix metering and will automatically switch to center-weighted metering. The aperture preferred mode, however, continues to work properly. The disadvantage is that you cannot see the aperture value in the viewfinder and have to look at the lens' aperture ring to determine it.

For non-AF lenses that do not have any kind of aperture transmission, such as adapters, bellows units, slide duplicators, and specialized lenses, a "-" will also appear in the viewfinder. The N90/F90 will automatically switch to "working aperture mode."

Working Aperture Mode

Working aperture mode is an aperture priority mode that calculates the exposure time AFTER the shutter release has been depressed, the lens closed to its selected aperture, and light falls onto the film plane. And while the exactness of the exposure time does not suffer, the exposure times displayed in the viewfinder and on the LCD panel do not mean anything. Since Matrix metering is not possible, the N90/F90 automatically uses center-weighted metering.

❐ **Example** - Let's assume that you are using a screw-mounted 400mm f/5.6 lens with a T-adapter. To focus, you have to open the lens fully to f/5.6. In this case, you can even use the autofocus focus assist. Before exposing the frame, you must manually adjust the aperture to the value you require, f/11 for example. You will notice this change (contrary to wide open metering) by a darkening of the viewfinder. At the moment of exposure, the N90/F90 measures the effective picture illumination in a few milliseconds and sets the exposure time it calculates as a result of this reading.

The disadvantages of the working aperture mode are the reduced ease of operation and the reduced speed. Additionally, actual exposure time is only displayed in the viewfinder and on the central LCD panel after the exposure.

Recommendations

❐ **Areas of application** - Aperture priority mode is useful in situations where depth of field (either large or small) is of utmost importance.

❐ **Depth of field preview** - The human eye has very limited depth of field adjustment and cannot focus close-up and on infinity at the same time. For that reason, it is not a dependable tool for judging depth of field. The depth of field preview button is, however. Located right next to the lens, your middle finger should touch it when holding the N90/F90. When in aperture priority or manual mode, press the button while looking in the viewfinder, and you will be able to see the scene's depth of field.

❐ **Appropriate lenses** - Any lens, generally from 28mm up, is suitable. Keep in mind, however, that if the lens does not have electrical contacts for transmitting aperture data, the working aperture mode will be used.

❐ **Appropriate films** - You must decide where and with how much light you are going to shoot. In churches or (secretly) in museums, it is better to use ISO 400 and get barely sharp shots at 1/60, than to use ISO 100 and get blurred images at 1/15. To shoot in theaters or at concerts (often not permitted), the same considerations apply.

I would personally only use ISO 1600 or even ISO 3200 if I could avoid long-exposure times and blurring problems by using them. If I am shooting on a tripod outside at night, however, I do prefer ISO 100 or 200 films to the more sensitive films. After all, the sharpness, grain, and color reproduction is simply better.

Error Warnings

There are two warnings which could potentially appear in the viewfinder and on the LCD: "HI" and "LO." See the section on shutter priority for a detailed explanation of these warnings.

Be aware that due to optical imperfections, circles often become ovals when shooting wide open with long shutter speeds.

Additionally, in situations where there is not enough light, the camera automatically switches into shutter preferred mode.

Reciprocity Failure

This is a phenomenon which causes film, during long exposures, to not react in a linear fashion to the light. In other words, the results of a ten minute exposure may not be twice those of a five minute exposure. Reciprocity failure generally starts occurring in all daylight balance films at about 1/15 second. Increased exposures are necessary to compensate for this effect. With the N90/F90, you do not have to worry about exposure times of up to 2 seconds, since Matrix metering tends to expose relatively dark subjects correctly. When using even longer exposure times, however, corrections become necessary. These can be set easily and exactly on the N90/F90. How much to correct depends on the film. You should either bracket or request a technical sheet from the film manufacturer giving reciprocity data.

Understanding Aperture Priority

After pre-selecting the aperture on the lens' aperture ring and activating the metering system by touching the shutter release, the camera's computer calculates the appropriate exposure time. Since the N90/F90 works with full-aperture metering, as do all other modern cameras, the diaphragm does not close to its actual working aperture for metering. To calculate the exposure time, the aperture setting of the lens is electronically transmitted to the CPU.

Manual Photography: Fully Manual Exposure Selection

In this mode, the N90/F90 essentially becomes a completely manually-operated camera. The user selects both shutter speed and aperture, based on the camera's light reading, or on a reading taken by a separate meter. In many cases, an experienced photographer using manual selection and center-weighted or spot metering can achieve better results than the N90/F90's automatic exposure systems.

Procedure

While holding down the MODE button, turn the command dial until "M" appears in the LCD. After this point, the aperture is set on the lens and the shutter speed is set with the command dial.

Compatible Lenses

All recent Nikkors are compatible, but for maximum ease of operation, use an AF-Nikkor.

Recommendations

❒ **Areas of application** - Generally, you would only use this mode in situations where you would rather not leave the decision making to the camera.

As cumbersome as manual methods are, they sometimes can be the best for subjects that are moving too quickly for the automatic modes to deal with. Consider soccer players clothed in white on a green field. Depending on the proportion of field to player in each of the 8 metering areas of the Matrix, the exposure could be correct, under-, or over-exposed. In a case like this, you can set the exposure values manually and avoid the risk of a poor image. Switch the camera to "M," frame a grey area (the field for example) and set the corresponding aperture and shutter speed. This exposure value will remain constant through the entire series of shots, assuming that the light conditions do not change drastically. The result is a set of consistently exposed images that are easily enlarged.

❒ **Appropriate lenses -** Any lens will work well in this mode, but those with relatively long focal lengths are generally preferred.

❒ **Appropriate films -** Use film of at least ISO 400. When the situation warrants, use ISO 1000.

❒ **Appropriate metering modes -** Even though Matrix metering works in manual mode, I feel this is a contradiction in itself. You either want to use auto-exposure or you want to measure and set your exposure on a very specific target. This does not coincide with an automatic exposure correction that happens "behind the photographer's back" without displaying its result.

Comparison with the Light Scale

Frame your subject and lightly touch the shutter release button. The appropriate aperture/time combination is displayed within 1/3 stop. To use this scale, change the aperture or shutter speed until it shows "0."

❒ **Example -** Let's assume that the exposure time is set at 1/125 second, the aperture at f/8, and the light scale shows +1. You can either leave the aperture at f/8 and change the exposure time to 1/250, or you can leave the exposure time unchanged and move the lens' aperture ring to f/11. In either case, you change the exposure time or aperture to reduce the exposure until the light scale shows "0."

Keep in mind that for every decrease in time, you have to open the lens one stop, and vice versa.

❒ **With non-AF lenses -** When using manual focus lenses, the camera automatically switches to center-weighted metering, and there is no aperture value shown in the viewfinder or on the central LCD. Regardless, the analog scale does show the correct exposure comparison. In this case, the aperture should be set wide open to focus and then closed down to the appropriate shooting value.

Targeted Metering

When metering the subject, you can make use of the metering rings marked on the viewing screen as aids. With contrasty subjects, e.g. back-lit, center-weighted metering might not do the trick. You either have to get so close to the subject that it just about fills the frame or switch to spot metering. The metered exposure value determined when the subject filled the frame can be set manually and you can now shoot the desired composition. The exposure will remain constant. Manual settings can hence be used as a permanent exposure storage method.

❒ **Choosing the metering point** - Areas that are grey or of medium reflection are best. Unusual reflective properties (black on black or white on white) require special exposure corrections. You will find more details in the "Basics of Exposure" chapter.

Manual Focus with Manual Exposure

The statement that autofocus photography is particularly fast is only completely true when the subject is in the center of the frame, and hence in the center of AF field. Even AF mode "C" does not have a chance if the subject is not in the center of the frame. Therefore, you must first frame the subject and store this focus setting. Only then can you select your composition and expose. All this can be done much faster manually with some practice. In these situations, there is a specific method to manual focusing:

❒ **Pre-selecting the distance** - Set your camera to AF mode "M" and focus on the area where the subject will appear at the time of exposure. You can use the AF focus aid to do this.

❒ **Pre-selecting the exposure** - With the help of the built-in light meter, select an aperture/shutter speed combination that will give enough depth of field, but still allow a short enough exposure. Because of the relatively small apertures that result from today's fast films, you have a fairly large focus area to play with.

❒ **Expose when you see it**: When something interesting happens at the pre-selected spot, depress the shutter release button. Your reaction time is all that stands between you and an exciting image.

Using the Sharpness Indicator

You can use the AF sharpness indicator to help you decide when to shoot. The sharpness symbol will appear whenever something appears in the selected focus plane. Exposing at that instant guarantees a sharp image. Manually pre-setting focus in conjunction with the AF focus indicator cannot be beaten in terms of speed. What takes the time in auto mode is not evaluating and displaying focus, but the motorized focusing function. Using this method, you avoid the latter.

An alternative method can be performed with the MF-26 Multi-function Back. Please see that section for details

The "Bulb" Setting

The name "bulb" ("B") goes back to the beginnings of photography, when shutters were pneumatically released with a rubber bladder: the shutter stayed open as long as there was pressure on the bulb. The internationally recognized "B" was derived from this.

❒ **Procedure -** In situations where an exposure time of 30 seconds is not adequate, switch to manual exposure mode and turn the control dial until "B" appears in the LCD. With this "exposure time," the shutter will remain open as long as the shutter release button is depressed. The remote trigger MC-20 is useful for this purpose. It can program exposure times from 1 second to 9 hours 59 min. 59 sec. without the danger of shaking the camera (can also function in T mode). Time exposures can also be programmed using the Multi-function Back MF-26. Please see that section for details.

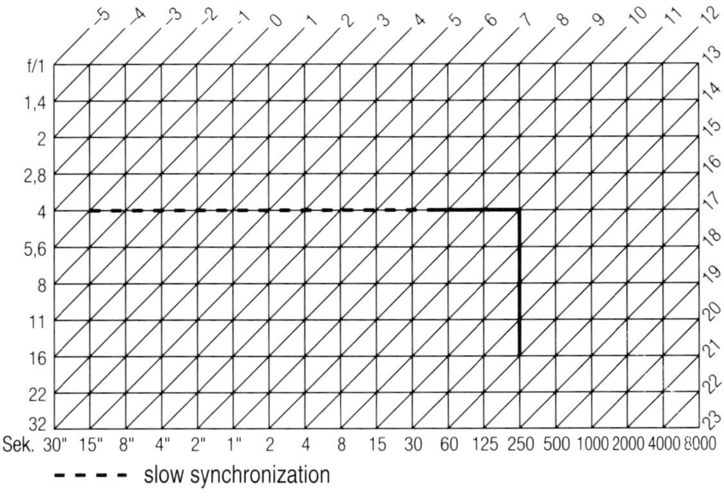

Overview of Flash Photography with the N90/F90

The N90/F90 has, in my opinion, the best flash automation of any camera on the market, even without the intricacies of the SB-25 flash unit. The only disadvantage is that with countless options, countless decisions must be made. I have tried very hard to explain the many options the N90/F90 offers in as simplified a manner as possible.

Nikon's TTL (through the lens) technology can only be utilized when using a Nikon flash unit with TTL capability, such as the SB-24 and SB-25.

TTL Flash in Multi-program Mode

The simplest way to use a flash with the N90/F90 is to set the camera to "P", metering to Matrix, and the mounted Nikon flash to TTL. The N90/F90 will automatically select the appropriate aperture and shutter speed and will calibrate the flash. Major exposure errors are just about impossible.

❒ **Aperture and exposure ranges -** The automatically selected aperture covers a range of f/4 to f/16. The selected shutter speed covers a range of 1/60 to 1/250 second. In "slow" mode, the exposure time can be as long as 30 seconds, depending on the subject's illumination.

❒ **Limits of the flash program mode -** If you want to select specific aperture values because of focus or depth of field considerations, you should use flash in conjunction with the aperture priority mode. If you want to have a lighter or darker background with fill flash, you should manually set the exposure time.

❒ **Backlit shots -** If, for example, you are photographing someone in front of a bright background, the N90/F90 can brighten the subject without the use of flash through Matrix metering. In these pictures, however, the subject will still be too dark, the background will be unnaturally bright, and the colors of the subject will not be very saturated. When using a flash, however, not only are the

⇦ **Fill-flash in multi-program mode.**

colors of the subject bright and saturated, but the background assumes a more natural illumination as well.

❐ **Flash with Ambient Light -** Unless you are shooting in a dark cellar at midnight, natural light adds a certain ambience to the image and should not be overpowered by the flash. With TTL flash, it will not be. This mode uses large apertures, relatively long exposure times, and very little flash (automatic minus correction) to provide correct illumination.

Flash in Aperture Priority Mode

In "A" mode, you can freely select the aperture and thereby control focus and depth of field while using flash.

❐ **Procedure -** Set the camera to "A," metering to Matrix, and the mounted Nikon flash to TTL. Select an aperture on the lens' aperture ring, and the exposure time will be automatically set between 1/60 and 1/250 second, depending on the ambient light.

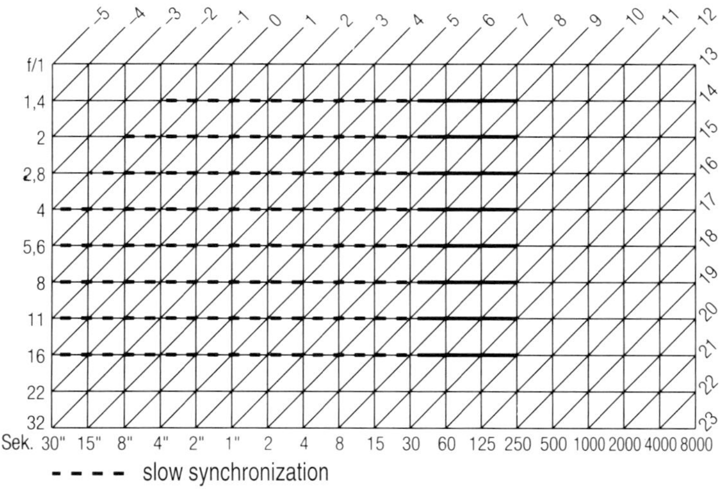

Fill-flash in aperture priority mode.

The flash will be calibrated by TTL during exposure. See also the "Large Subjects" and "Varying Background Illumination" sections in this chapter.

❒ **Aperture and exposure ranges -** The pre-selectable aperture range covers f/1.4 to f/16 (according to my tests, f/32 is also possible with certain film sensitivities). The automatically set shutter speed varies from 1/60 to 1/250 second, depending on subject illumination. Exposures up to 30 seconds are possible in the "slow" mode.

Flash in Shutter Priority Mode

In this mode, you can freely select any shutter speed from 1/250 to 30 seconds. Since the danger of blurring due to movement by the photographer or the subject decreases from 1/60 second up, I do not see any advantages to using the shutter preferred mode for fill flash or normal flash photography. Even stationary objects are are not recommended subjects in shutter priority mode because of the importance of depth of field. However, the shutter priority mode is useful to create desired motion blur effects.

❒ **Procedure -** Set the camera to "S," the metering system to Matrix, and the mounted Nikon flash to TTL. Using the command dial, select a shutter speed between 1/250 and 30 seconds. An appropriate aperture will be selected depending on the ambient light. The flash will be calibrated according to the TTL. The result of this flash mode is a good correspondence between background and foreground illumination.

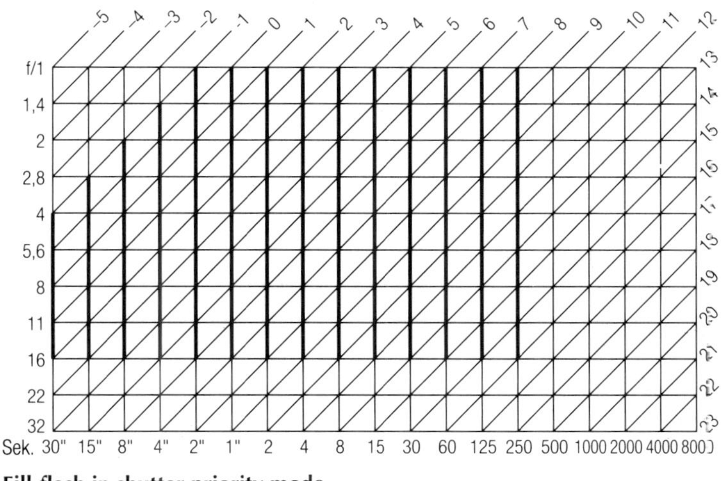

Fill-flash in shutter priority mode.

❐ **Aperture and exposure ranges -** In flash shutter priority mode, a shutter speed of 1/250 to 30 seconds can be selected. The automatically set aperture technically covers a range between f/1 and f/16, although I managed to reach f/32 in my testing.

Flash in Fully Manual Mode

In this mode, you can freely set shutter speeds from 1/250 to 30 seconds (with the SB-25 and FP, even 1/4000 second) and apertures between f/1.4 and f/32 using the manual exposure comparison. You can control background versus foreground illumination depending on metering method and the framed part of the subject. And by carefully selecting the shutter speed/aperture combination, you can create motion effects ranging from freeze to motion blur.

TTL Flash in Fully Manual Mode

In this mode, you can freely set shutter speeds from 1/250 to 30 seconds (with the SB-25 and FP, even 1/4000 second) and apertures between f/1.4 and f/32 using the manual exposure comparison. You can control background versus foreground illumination depending on metering method and the framed part of the subject. And by carefully selecting the shutter speed/aperture combination, you can create motion effects ranging from freeze to motion blur.

❐ **Procedure -** Select exposure mode "M" and metering mode Matrix, spot, or center-weighted. Set the flash to TTL. Frame the section of the subject on which the illumination balance should based. Using either the built-in or a handheld meter, select an exposure time from 1/250 to 30 seconds along with an appropriate aperture. With these settings made, the flash will be controlled by the TTL system during the exposure.

Fully Manual Flash Operation

Here, the TTL system is deactivated and you have full reign over the control of the flash and camera's operation. The downside is that you must be experienced enough to calculate correct exposure values.

The flash unit has a given guide number. The photographer selects an aperture appropriate to the distance to the subject. The only real advantage of fully manual mode is that all lenses and flash units (as long as they are compatible) can be used.

Please be aware that the following explanations apply only to flash units that are mounted on the camera and not to studio setups where various flash units with different outputs can be positioned independent of the camera.

❐ **Procedure** - Set the camera to exposure mode "M" and select an exposure time of 1/250 second or longer. If you are using a Nikon flash, set it to mode "M" as well as to the appropriate ISO. By reading the flash unit's scale, determine the f-stop which corresponds to the shutter speed which you have set. Set the lens' aperture ring to this f-stop and depress the shutter release button.

❐ **The Verdict** - Since the guide numbers of various flash units vary and because the reflective properties of the image's background play an important role in the final image, quality pictures taken using only the guide number are few and far between. It is much safer to work with a flash meter whether in a studio or "on location." As an alternative, you can always bracket the exposure by simply changing the aperture, guaranteeing at least one good picture. But because of the N90/F90's well-designed flash automation, situations in which a manual flash is preferred have all but disappeared.

TTL Flash with Non-AF Nikkors

While using AF lenses is the preferred method, it is possible to use a conventional-focus lens with Nikon's advanced flash units.

❐ **Procedure** - Set the camera, as described above, to aperture priority mode and either spot or center-weighted metering. Set the flash to TTL and the lens to the desired aperture. The situation's ambient light (the contrast between fore- and background in backlit situations) will be automatically considered, and the TTL system will adjust the exposure time and flash duration.

TTL Multi-Sensor Flash

This is a feature that is automatic and requires no input from you Regardless of the exposure and metering mode you have selected (Matrix is preferred), Multi-Sensor flash is enabled. The only requirement is that you use an AF, AF-D or AI-P Nikkor lenses.

❐ **Explanation** - With Multi-Sensor flash in program mode, the aperture and shutter speed are automatically set before the exposure, according to the camera's meter reading. After the shutter is released and the flash triggered, the TTL control (regardles of the metering method chosen) uses a five-field Multi-Sensor reading to determine the necessary flash intensity. Extremely reflective properties of a subject are therefore automatically compensated for.

TTL Multi-Sensor with Monitor Preflash

This is another fully automatic feature, activated only when using AF or AI-P Nikkors in conjunction with Nikon's SB-25.

❒ **Explanation -** Here, the SB-25 sends a series of invisible measuring flashes that the Multi-Sensor evaluates as soon as the shutter is released. The flash unit uses this information to determine the situation's spatial distribution and the reflective properties in order to select the appropriate flash intensity.

3D Multi-Sensor with Monitor Preflash

This is an even more specialized yet totally automatic feature. It is enabled only when using type D Nikkors in conjunction with the SB-25.

❒ **Explanation -** Unlike the 2D system described above, this feature also takes into account the distance to the subject. The measuring flashes accurately account for off-center subjects and extremely reflective properties of the surroundings.

Flash-controlled Exposure Compensation

The exposure of any given image can be adjusted with the flash instead of the camera.

When making compensations with the camera body, the entire exposure (aperture, shutter speed, and flash duration) is affected in all flash exposure modes. Both the foreground and background, therefore, become brighter or darker. It is important to note that a change in film sensitivity also changes the guide number and hence the maximum flash distance.

Focal lengths from about 18mm to 21mm along with apertures of f/8 or better yet, f/11 are ideal for landscape images; the typical wide-angle perspective gives ample depth of field. While Matrix metering will suffice in images like the one on top , the experienced pro will bracket a scene like the one on the bottom. Pictures: Wolf Huber ➪

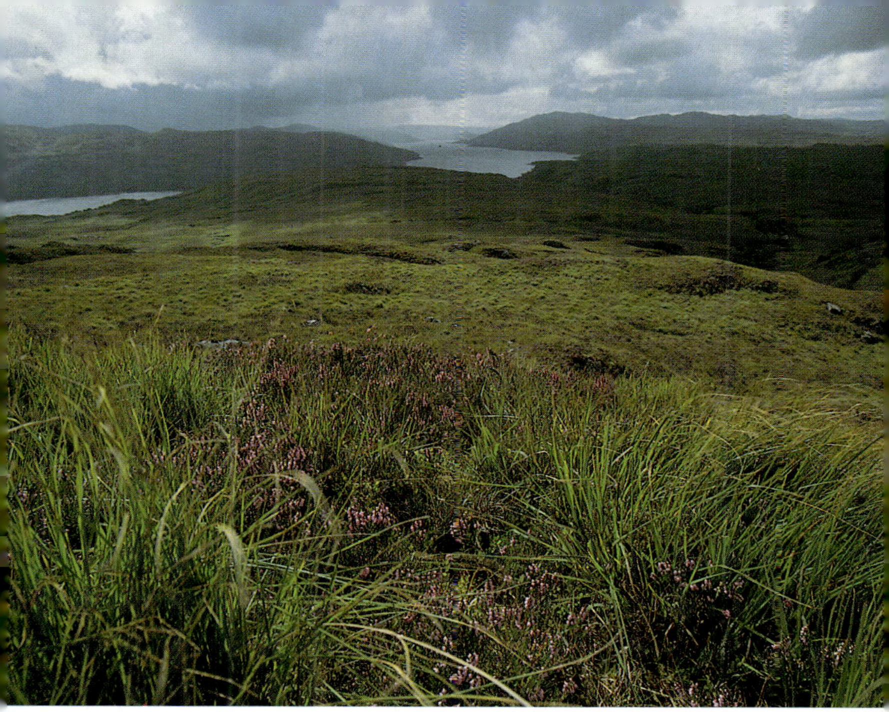

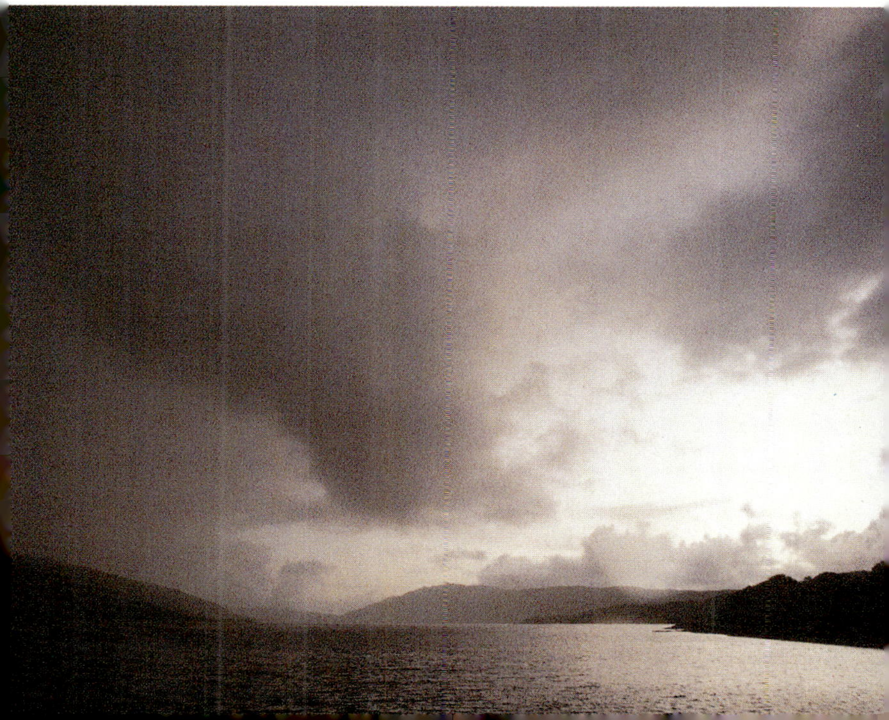

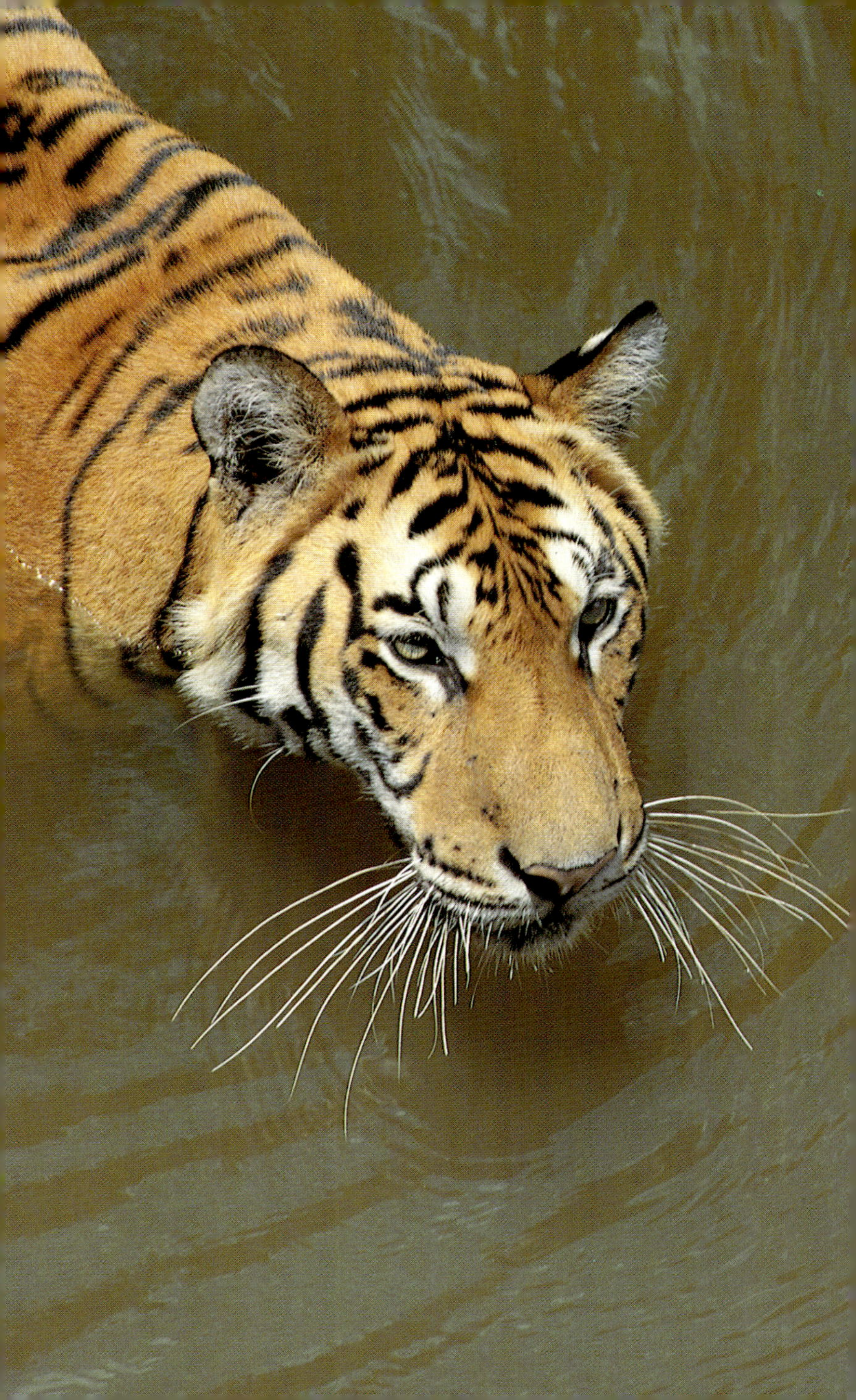

With flash exposure compensation, on the other hand, the flash duration can be changed indepencently of the aperture and shutter speed. Therefore, the illumination of the foreground and the background can also be changed independently.

❐ **Manual correction -** This is possib e only when using a Nikon SB-24 or SB-25. Manual correction, like its automatic counterpart, only affects the flash duration. It can be set on the flash units themselves, from -3 EV to +1 EV.

Manual correction is also possible with other Nikon System flash units when using the MF-26 Multi-control Back (the MF-26 overrides the SB-24 and SB-25 when used with them). Activating the manual flash correction mode automatically turns the auto mode off.

With automatic flash bracketing, the camera shoots a series of exposures, changing only the flash duration in increments selected by the user. This last option is possible only when using the MF-26.

Selecting a Metering Mode

In all auto-flash modes, the selected metering method reads only the ambient light. Automatic TTL flash control occurs independently after the shutter is released, with a slightly center-weighted bias. When AF Nikkors are used, a five-field Multi-Sensor reading will be taken.

❐ **Matrix metering -** Only Matrix metering considers ambient light and subject contrast required for perfect exposures. In auto-flash modes, it is the only sensible choice, but only available when using AF Nikkors.

❐ **Center-weighted metering -** This method does not measure the ambient light and subject illumination as accurately as does

Matrix metering. It is, however, the logical choice when an AF Nikkor is unavailable.

Because the tiger will not go swimming twice, there is no time to focus and meter. With a telephoto zoom at 200mm, autofocus, and multi-program mode, such snap-shots are usually successful.
Picture: Heribert Mindl

❒ **Spot metering** - This option only makes sense when manually setting the exposure on a large subject. If the exposure is set on the camera such that the distant subject area is normally bright anyway, use of the flash will serve to lighten the foreground.

Controlling the Flash

Now that you are familiar with the fundamentals of Nikon flash photography, let's go over the most important control features. For a more in-depth look at Nikon's most modern units, the SB-24 and SB-25, separate books on the subject are available.

Automatic Flash Indicator

If the subject's illumination (based on the film sensitivity and the subject's brightness) has an EV value of less than 10, the green flash diode in the viewfinder will illuminate, prompting you to use flash.

Automatic Fill-flash Indicator

If the subject contrast (frame center vs. background) is greater than 1 f/stop, the green flash diode in the viewfinder illuminates, prompting you to use fill-flash. In program TTL mode with Matrix metering, the camera will determine exactly how much flash is necessary for a perfect exposure.

Flash Status

When the flash unit is attached and turned on, an indicator will glow in the viewfinder. This indicator relays a variety of information, depending on the situation.

❒ **Fully charged** - If the flash symbol diode in the viewfinder glows red for at least 2 seconds, the flash is fully charged. When you are shooting a series of images, the flash will fire with each exposure, although it may not be fully charged.

❒ **Insufficient power** - If the flash symbol flashes repeatedly or goes out altogether after an exposure, the flash was too weak to properly expose the photograph. You can remedy the situation by opening the lens (in "A" or "M" mode) or getting closer to the subject.

❒ **Poor contact** - The flash diode will also blink if there is a bad connection between the flash unit and the camera. Take the flash unit off and remount it, being sure to tighten the securing ring.

Test Flash

It is possible to fire most flash units without exposing film by pressing the test button. On most Nikon flash units, it is the glowing red light on the back of the flash. When it is pressed, the flash's computer reads the flash. If the control indicator on the flash illuminates after the test, the flash is powerful enough for a TTL-controlled exposure.

Using Multiple TTL Flash Units

You can take automatic flash shots using several flash units with the N90/F90. With some experience, you can lighten backgrounds, simulate backlighting, and a great deal more. Drastic exposure errors are impossible, thanks to TTL automation.

Appropriate Flash Units

With multiple flash photography, you should use only contemporary Nikon System flash units. The SB-23, for instance, is a good choice for a main flash, but not as an auxiliary flash unit. Non-Nikon flash units that are supposedly Nikon-compatible should only be used with a written performance guarantee from the manufacturer.

Flash Combinations

You cannot use an unlimited number of flash units because the camera's electronics can become overloaded. Each Nikon System flash unit has a numerical power rating. For instance, the SB-20 has a power rating of 9, the SB-22 is rated at 6, the SB-23 at 4, and the SB-24 and SB-25 are rated at 1. The total system must not have a power rating greater than 20. You can figure out the various combinations.

System Overload

If too many flash units are combined, you may not be able to fire the shutter. To reset the camera, disconnect all flash units and turn each of them off and then on individually. It may also help to use one less unit.

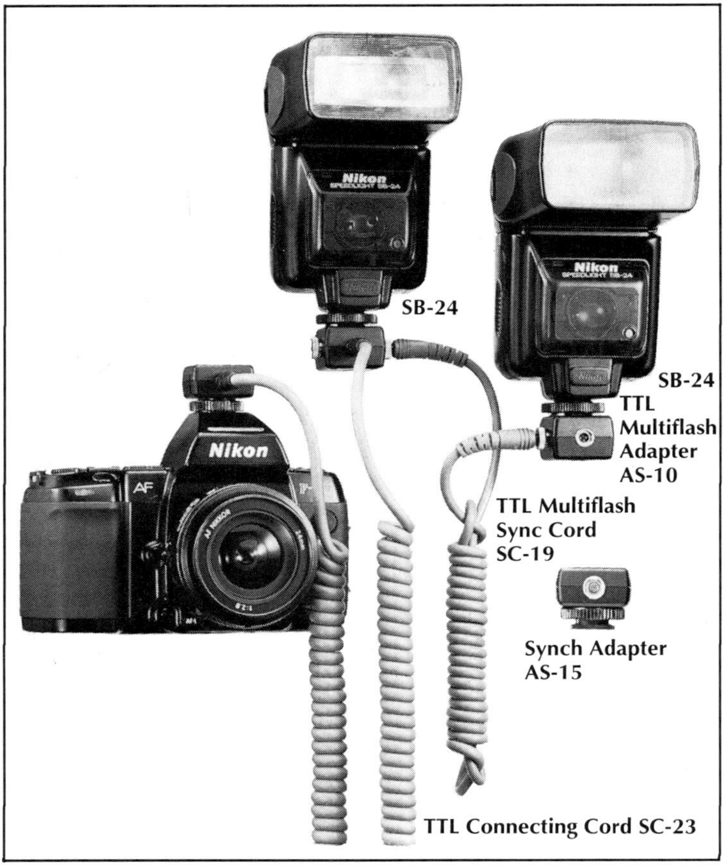

Multiple-flash setups, such as the one shown here with an N8008/F-801, are possible with the N90/F90 and the SB-25 flash.

Necessary Accessories

There are relatively few accessories absolutely necessary for multiple flash photography. Besides the flash units themselves, you will need one TTL multi-flash adapter (AS-10) for each unit, one TTL flash shoe adapter cord (SC-17), and a few TTL extension cords (SC-18 or SC-19). If one of the units is mounted in the camera's hot shoe, however, the SC-17 cord is not necessary.

Helpful Hints

You must observe a few rules to assure simultaneous flashing of each connected flash unit. The first rule is to use only Nikon System flash units; mixing units of various manufacturers can lead not only to misfiring but also to damage of the camera and the flash units.

Additionally, all flash units should have similar discharge characteristics. This does not apply, however, to Nikon System flash units with different guide numbers. In reality, guide numbers make no difference as long as you use the highest power unit as the main light. It is logical that the less powerful units should be used to illuminate the background, or as fill and accent lights.

Keep in mind, however, that the fill-flash mode reads the ambient light before the flash. Since the additional flash units illuminate the background, rendering this reading useless, it is recommended to manually expose, using a hand-held meter.

The Limits of Flash Automation

While Nikon's TTL system may seem to be foolproof, there are several things that you should keep in mind whenever using a flash unit in conjunction with the N90/F90.

Limits of Metering

As far as the ambient exposure reading before the actual exposure is concerned, the same limits apply as with Matrix, center-weighted or spot metering.

Danger of Over-exposure

If the distance to the subject is very small as compared to the guide number of the flash and film speed, the danger of over-exposure is particularly great.

In aperture priority or manual mode, the only solution is to stop down the lens or use a slower film (lower ISO number). As an alternative, you can use a neutral density filter in front of the flash unit. As a last resort, you can use white facial tissue, typewriter paper, or any other white paper to reduce the flash output.

Danger of Under-exposure

This exists if the subject distance is so great that the flash's total light output is inadequate. This maximum flash distance, which decreases with smaller apertures, corresponds with the reach of the flash unit in a manual setting. Even the best flash system cannot produce more than "full flash." If output is not enough, your options are to move closer to the subject, use a faster film, or open the lens further in aperture preferred or manual modes.

Unusual Reflection

Problems can arise when using flash on subjects that have unusual reflective properties. A bride dressed in white standing in front of a white wall will appear too dark, and a widow dressed in black in front of a black coffin will appear too light. To compensate for these discrepancies, you must set the camera and flash to "M" and manually compensate.

Film Speeds and Aperture Range

In order for a flash picture to be properly exposed, the entire scene must fall into the effective range of the flash unit. This range, for any given flash, is dependent on the speed of the film being used and the maximum aperture of the lens.

❒ **Film -**The N90/F90's flash modes can only be used with film speeds from ISO 25 to ISO 1000.

❒ **Aperture -** Maximum aperture will vary with different lenses. The larger the maximum aperture, the larger the range.

Correction Range

Setting normal exposure corrections has the same effect as using different film speeds. The N90/F90's automatically changes the range of the exposure correction values depending on the circumstances.

The Verdict

Despite these few downfalls, there is no doubt that the N90/F90, especially when used with the SB-25 and type D Nikkors, can produce flash pictures with much more consistent quality than can any of its pedecessors.

The Appropriate Mode

Depending on the situation in which you find yourself, you must choose an appropriate exposure mode. Here are a few guidelines.

Program

In situations with pronounced ambient light, like cases with backlighting, a balance between foreground and background can be achieved by selecting a combination of aperture and shutter speed according to the background's brightness. The combination of Matrix metering, program mode, and fill-flash mode will work well in these cases.

Manual Exposure

As an alternative, you can achieve equally good (if not better) results with several manual exposure combinations.

❒ **With fill-flash and spot metering:** Useful in situations where the the background is lit with sufficient ambient light.

❒ **With SLOW mode -** A good alternative for subjects against black backgrounds with little ambient light.

Since the light that is emitted by the flash decreases with the square of the distance, you will find that the background looks like a "black hole" if it is too far behind the subject. A typical situation is a large, dimly-lit room. With a pre-selected aperture in manual or aperture priority modes, the camera will select a correspondingly long exposure time. Do not forget to use a tripod and a remote shutter release to avoid camera shake.

Special Flash Functions

There are several photographic options that become possible when using the N90/F90 in conjunction with a modern Nikon System flash unit.

To Control Background Brightness

Depending on the situation, you may or may not want the foreground and background to be equally lit. To separate the main subject from the background, it is sometimes advantageous to create a darker or lighter background.

❒ **Procedure -** Using manual exposure mode, select a shutter speed appropriate for the lens' focal length and the situation (between 1/60 and 1/250 second). Read the main subject with spot or center-weighted metering and set the aperture as if you were not using a flash. By stopping down a few stops, you will achieve a darker background. The reverse is true if you open the diaphragm. Bracket exposures to achieve the desired result.

❒ **Foreground vs. Background -** The respective brightness of foreground and background can be varied by changing the exposure correction and flash correction in opposite directions. For example, set the camera to +1 EV and the flash to -1 EV. Once again, bracket exposures to attain optimal results.

To Control Depth of Field

In principle, you can create a sharp or fuzzy background at will by simply changing the aperture in "A" or "M" modes. This is only possible, however, if the background is relatively close to the main subject (no more than twice the subject's distance from the camera). If it is too far, the light intensity falls off noticeably and a change of aperture affects not only the depth of field but also the brightness of the background.

❒ **With long exposure times -** First, set the aperture according to the desired depth of field. Set the exposure time according to the description above "controlling background brightness." A flower in a relatively dark forest would appear in front of a black background when using a large aperture, as required shutter speeds of 1/60 or 1/250 second. Longer exposure times, on the other hand, result in a brighter background.

❒ **With extremely short (FP) exposure times -** If you want to separate the subject from a relatively bright background by using a shallow depth of field, you need a large aperture. With normal flash durations, however, the background will appear unnaturally bright because the flash will not sync at times faster than 1/250 second (on older cameras 1/60 second). But with the FP function of the N90/F90 and SB-25, shorter sync times are possible. Set the camera body to manual exposure mode, the SB-25 to "M," and the "M" button to FP. Then, select the aperture appropriate to the depth of field you desire. Set a shutter speed up to 1/4000 second after taking a spot reading of the background. Since the N90/F90 and the SB-25 work without TTL in FP mode, you must strictly adhere to the distance range, as indicated by the SB-25's digital readout.

For a Blurred Effect

Even with flash, you can carefully control motion effects. The sharp image created by the relatively short flash duration can be overlaid with blurred motion resulting from a long exposure. This can lead to some very interesting effects.

❒ **Procedure** - Set the N90/F90 to shutter priority mode, the flash to TTL, and select a shutter speed corresponding to the blur effect you would like to achieve. Similar effects can be produced with weak ambient light in program mode and SLOW or with manual exposure setting and slow shutter speeds.

❒ **Example** - Let's take a shutter speed of 1/8 second as an example. During the approximately 1/1000 second during which the flash is actually illuminated, only the flash's light will be of consequence. During the rest of the exposure, ambient light will expose the film. If your subject is in motion, a blurred image will add itself to the flash's sharp image on the frame. A similar effect results when the exposure is so long that you yourself move: a sharp image from the flash with a halo of movement around it. Without doubt, this is an area with a great deal of room for experimentation.

For Natural Motion

When using longer shutter speeds, switch to REAR curtain sync. This means that the flash will be synchronized with the rear shutter curtain (this is a bit of a misnomer; the N90/F90 actually has blades instead of curtains). In other words, the ambient light exposure occurs before the flash is triggered. While conventional synchronization causes objects to unnaturally "push" their motion blur ahead of themselves, this method allows the object to "pull" its motion trail behind it.

❒ **Procedure** - Put the camera into "S" or "M" mode and select a shutter speed that will give you the desired amount of blur. If you are using an SB-24 or SB-25, select rear synchronization on the flash unit itself. Otherwise, select it using the FLASH button on the N90/F90's button cluster.

To Freeze Motion

The flash unit can be used to freeze the motion of your subject.

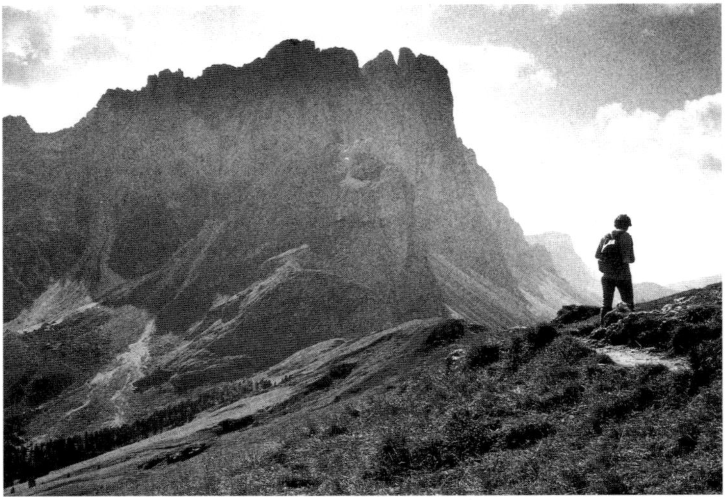

Mountain pictures are usually taken with wide-angle lenses to get an "overview" scene. In order not to have the mountains appear tiny, the foreground must be carefully considered during composition. ⇧

By using a lens with a focal length between about 80mm and 200mm in addition to a high vantage point, converging lines are prevented. Here, the grave stones are placed comfortingly in front of the vine-overgrown ruin in the background. ⇨

Everyone has seen the photograph of a bullet ripping through a playing card. The idea here is the same.

❒ **Procedure -** Set the camera to "M" and shutter speed to "bulb." Adjust the lens to the desired aperture. If the flash unit, set to TTL, is fired in low light or light or in complete darkness, the subject will be exposed during the relatively short flash duration.

❒ **With bright ambient light -** If there is a good deal of light present and you wish to use fill-flash on a moving object, it is difficult to use normal flash sync. A sharp flash image will have a blurred image on top of it, even at 1/250 second. In this case, only short sync mode FP will help.

Set SB-25 to "M" and FP on the "M" button. Then select a shut-

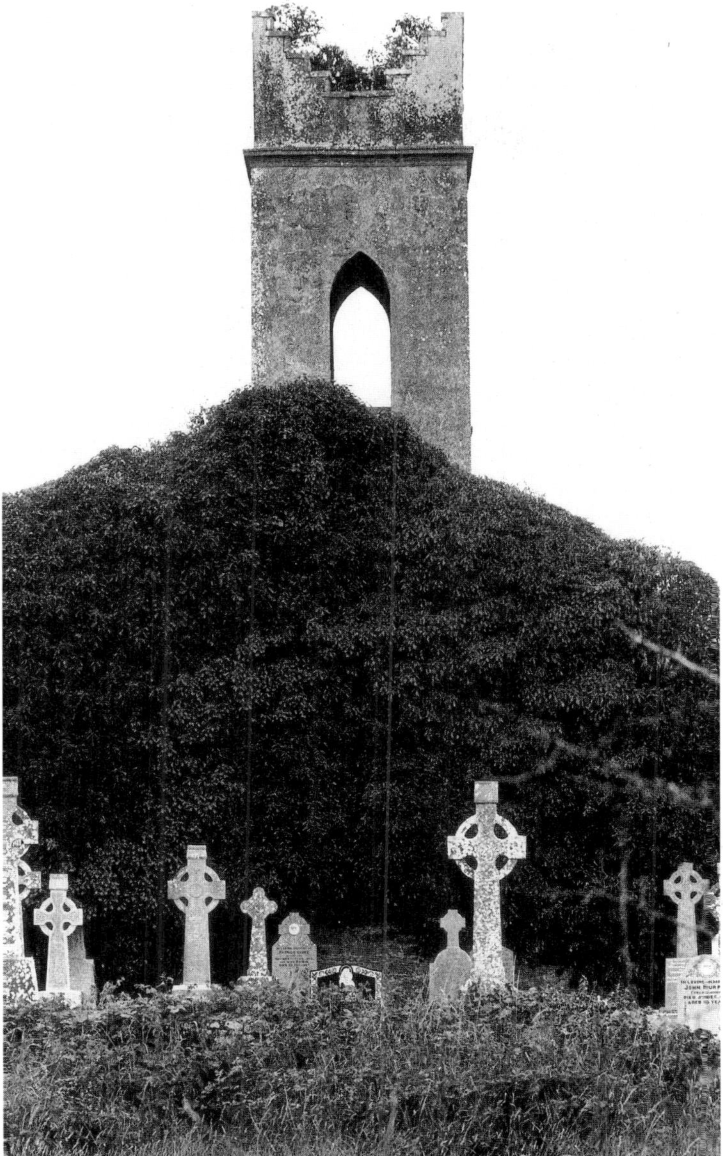

ter speed of up to 1/4000 second and an aperture that will yield the desired depth of field.

Again, because the TTL system is disabled in FP mode, you must adhere to the distance range, as indicated on the flash unit's read-out.

To Separate Motion

The SB-24 and SB-25 flash units have a strobe function which generates a series of very short flashes, one after the other, just like a strobe light. This means that any movement will be separated into a series of sharp partial images. Strobe pictures enable the analysis of fast movements in sports and science, and produce pictures that are generally just very interesting to look at.

❒ **Procedure -** Set the N90/F90 to manual exposure and select an appropriate shutter speed/aperture combination. Now set the main selector switch on the flash to strobe, indicated by three lightning bolts in a box. Now you must select the time between flashes (frequency) from 1 second to 1/50 second, the number of flashes (1 to 160), and the flash power from 1/1 to 1/64. Possible combinations depend on flash power.

For example, with 1/8 power and a frequency of 1-7 Hz, 20 flashes can be made in a row. With 1/64 power, 160 flashes are possible.

Read the aperture indicated by the flash and set this on the lens. With a dark, steady background and little ambient light, strobe images work very well.

Studio Flash

Studio photography enables you to go ahead with your assignment, regardless of unpredictable ambient lighting conditions. Additionally, it is necessary when the lighting must be "150%" of what the photographer or client requires. Studio lighting is an exacting art form, and really requires a book of its own. For that reason, the following is just a very brief overview of this multi-faceted topic.

Desired Composition Through Flash Setup

This is accomplished by using several units with different outputs and the appropriate generators. With studio shots, you have the opportunity to use a wide variety of reflectors and light sources like glaring spotlights or soft "hazylights" to create effects ranging from hard sunlight to the soft illumination from a north-facing window. All this is possible with a power output that does not necessitate opening the lens, even with low sensitivity film.

Since the duration of most studio flash units is around 1/300 second or shorter, motion is easily frozen and you can work quite easily without a tripod. In addition to active light sources, you also have access to reflective panels and diffusers in the studio. In order to judge the lighting, studio flash units have a halogen modeling light that changes its output proportionally to the flash power. This means that the illumination can be examined beforehand, unlike when using camera-mounted flash units that leave you, quite literally, in the dark. It is obvious that not just any automated flash mode will fit the bill in this exacting situation. After all, each flash unit is assigned a different output or effect and camera-controlled flash output would not be able to take all these variables into account.

Manual Flash Exposure Metering

After all the variables have been set on the various flash units, the camera's aperture is determined by firing test flashes. To do this, use a flash meter at the subject, pointed in the camera's direction, to measure incident light. With this reading, you have the total of all direct and indirect light hitting the subject at the time of exposure. Provided that the film sensitivity and shutter speed were correctly set on the meter, the correct aperture can be read off it and set directly on the camera's lens.

Remote Triggering

While the flash is normally triggered by a long cable that is plugged into the N90/F90's flash sync terminal, an alternative is to use a small, hot shoe flash pointed at the ceiling to trigger other flash units, connected to photocells.

Another more advanced method of cordless flash triggering is the use of infrared triggering devices. These are superior to visible light triggers because they are unaffected by stray light from other sources. The Wein company makes several infrared flash triggering systems that enable you to trigger multiple units at the same time. The unit attached to the camera triggers all other Wein units simultaneously. Multi-channel units even allow you to selectively trigger certain flashes independently of the others. This is by far the most elegant solution to the off-camera flash situation.

Special Flash Situations

You will undoubtedly, from time to time, find yourself using flash in a variety of specialized situations. Here are some suggestions for dealing with a few of these situations.

Interior Architecture

In these situations, the power of your flash must be directly proportional to the size of the room. A guide number of 100 is no luxury.

Since you will probably be using a wide-angle lens, it is a good idea to also use a wide-angle diffuser on the flash unit itself. This accessory will, of course, reduce the effective flash output. The SB-25 with the zoom reflector is ideal for focal lengths down to 24mm (with the diffuser to 20mm).

It is also advisable to use slave units placed outside the image area to illuminate the corners of very large rooms.

❒ **Helpful hint -** Use economical units that can be threaded directly into normal lighting fixture sockets.

Unnatural Faces

If the faces in your flash pictures turn out looking unnaturally pale, invest in a flash diffuser. These are available at most all camera stores, and attach to the flash with Velcro®. In a pinch, you can use an index card and a rubber band to achieve the same effect. This is usually unnecessary with the N90/F90 and modern Nikon System flash units, since the TTL system automatically determines the correct flash intensity.

Slide Duplication

Flash units have become very useful in slide duplication. Unfortunately, the TTL flash control system might not be suitable to correctly expose the very sensitive Kodak slide duplicating film. It is best to use an ISO setting of 6, center-weighted TTL flash control, and even then take a few test shots.

The flash exposure can be modified by changing the distance to the slide or by adding neutral density filters in front of the flash. Additionally, manual flash corrections between -3 and +1 EV are also ideal for this purpose. For the necessary color correction in slide duplication, it is recommended that you acquire a CC filter set.

Snapshots

Whether it is a birthday party, Johnny under the Christmas tree, or a corporate anniversary party, most of your pictures will be snapshots. They are generally taken indoors at a distance of around 5-15 feet.

Focal lengths between about 28mm and 100mm are best suited to this purpose. With a flash unit guide number 100 and films of ISO 100 or 200, practically all of these shots will turn out perfectly. When using direct flash, make sure the subject is not too deep. The foreground and the background will appear too bright and too dark, respectively, because of the inverse square rule. This is particularly noticeable on exposure-sensitive slide films.

If you can, use an indirect, or bounced, flash. Most of Nikon's Sppedlites have built-in bounce capability. That is, the head can be tilted to bounce the light off a relatively low ceiling. Be careful, though. If the ceiling is any color but white, that color will tint the rest of the picture.

Macro Photography

Macro shots are generally best done with off-camera flash units All contemporary Nikon System flashes, when used with the multi-flash cable or adapter, are well suited to this purpose. Should the flash output prove too high, you can always add neutral density filters or simply some typewriter paper.

Minimum aperture with macro photography in TTL flash mode:

		Film Speed	
Flash Distance	**ISO 50**	**ISO 100**	**ISO 200**
9.8" (25 cm)	f/11	f/16	f/22
19.6" (50 cm)	f/5.6	f/ 8	f/11
		Minimum Aperture	

Nikon recommends using a minimum aperture for flash distances less than 25 inches. If a larger aperture is selected, the TTL System may not have enough time to correctly adjust the flash.

Portraiture and Product Photography

Studio portraits and product (tabletop) shots usually require a high flash output since the necessary degree of sharpness requires the use of slow films. Take care to provide even lighting; shadows or hard contrast are disturbing if not properly placed.

❒ **One flash unit** - You can cover a surprising amount of applications with only one flash unit. Adding an umbrella to the setup transforms a standard flash into a large, soft light source. An additional white or silver reflector (the Domke company makes some of the most versatile) can help lighten shadows.

❒ **Multiple flash units** - You can work even more precisely with several flash units; having three in a studio will cover most any circumstance. Normally, the strongest flash is fired nearly to straight-on as the main light source. Specialized diffuser panels, such as those made by Domke, do wonders with otherwise harsh lighting. A second, weaker unit can be used as background illumination or as a bottom light, and the third can be positioned to create accents.

As modeling lights are very useful but somewhat extravagant for a basic studio, two cheap clamp reflector sockets with 60W bulbs are an economical alternative.

❒ **Helpful hint** - Build a light tent out of tracing paper or diffuser material and use one flash unit on either side.

Large Subjects

You will quickly discover that very few subjects are flat; the vast majority have at least minimal depth. Imagine a long wedding buffet: if you select the aperture according to the center of the table, the bride in the foreground will be too bright, the groom at the other end will be too dark, while only the relatively unimportant center is properly exposed.

Even flash bounced off the white ceiling in manual mode is a game of chance in this situation. To find the correct exposure would require bracketing. That, in turn, requires time that you probably don't have. Using TTL mode in this situation eliminates all of this hassle.

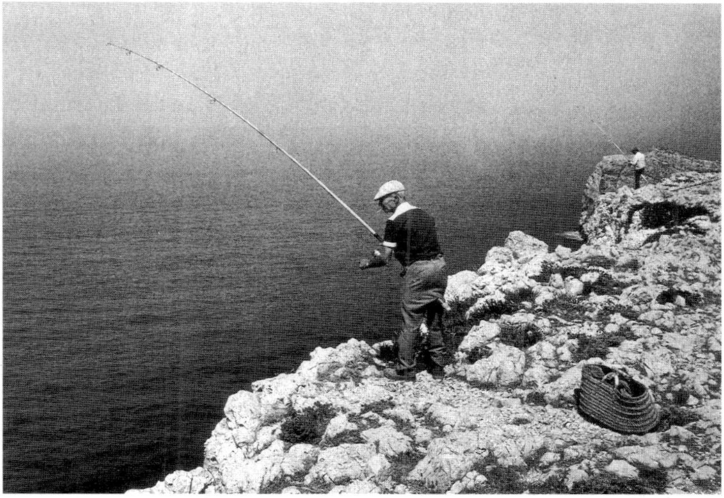

The fisherman in Algarve was photographed at close range with the a 35mm wide-angle lens.

Copy Photography

This is best done on a copy stand with two equally powered flash units mounted at a 45 degree angle. The distance from the lights for subjects up to 8 x 11 inches should be about one yard. Diffusers in front of the flash units are also recommended in this application.

Dealing with Red-eye

Notorious red-eye can be blamed on the camera-mounted flash unit. If the flash axis and lens axis are almost the same, the light reflected off the red retina becomes visible. If there is a significant distance between the lens and flash axes, however, the red light is reflected out of the image area. Diffusing the flash is one solution, but it reduces the flash intensity. A better alternative is the use of a flash bracket, such as those manufactured by Stroboframe. These brackets raise the flash high above the camera, effectively eliminating red-eye.

Lastly, remember that using SB-25 with the N90/F90 makes available the preflash option. This works fairly well, but is simply not as professional as the other methods.

Sport and Action Photography

Generally, flash photography is strictly forbidden in sporting arenas. If, however, you are in a situation where flash is permitted, use a telephoto lens and fast film. When using a flash, the N90/F90 can accommodate films with speeds of up to around ISO 1000.

Compatible Flash Units

From the large range of Nikon System flashes, the following are to be recommended for use with the N90/F90 due to their integrated AF illuminators: SB-20, SB-22, SB-23, SB-24 and SB-25.

If you seldom use flash, I would recommend the fairly economical and easy-to-use SB-23. If flash photography is part of your day-to-day routine, however, invest in the amazing new SB-25. It is state-of-the-art and cannot be beaten in usefulness with the N90/F90.

The SB-25

This flash unit incorporates all of Nikon's technological advancements available at this time. Here are a few of the SB-25's most important features:

Despite the fact that the SB-25 was designed for use with the N90/F90 (preflash can only be used with this camera), it is compatible with all SLR cameras in the Nikon line. Furthermore, it is, in my opinion, easier to use than its predecessor, the SB-24. Additionally, it has a motorized zoom reflector that automatically sets itself between 24mm and 85mm when using AF lenses.

A built-in diffuser is effective for lenses down to 20mm, and a built-in reflector allows you to travel without an index card in your camera bag.

The SB-25's built-in illuminator provides light to Nikon AF systems when there is otherwise not enough with which to focus. When using the SB-25 in conjunction with the N90/F90, F4, N8008/F-801, or N6006/F-601, you have the option of rear-curtain synchronization. When using it with older, manual cameras, set the flash unit to "M" and use it like any other flash.

TTL and fill-flash modes make the SB-25 extremely versatile, basically insuring perfect exposures every time. The stroboscopic

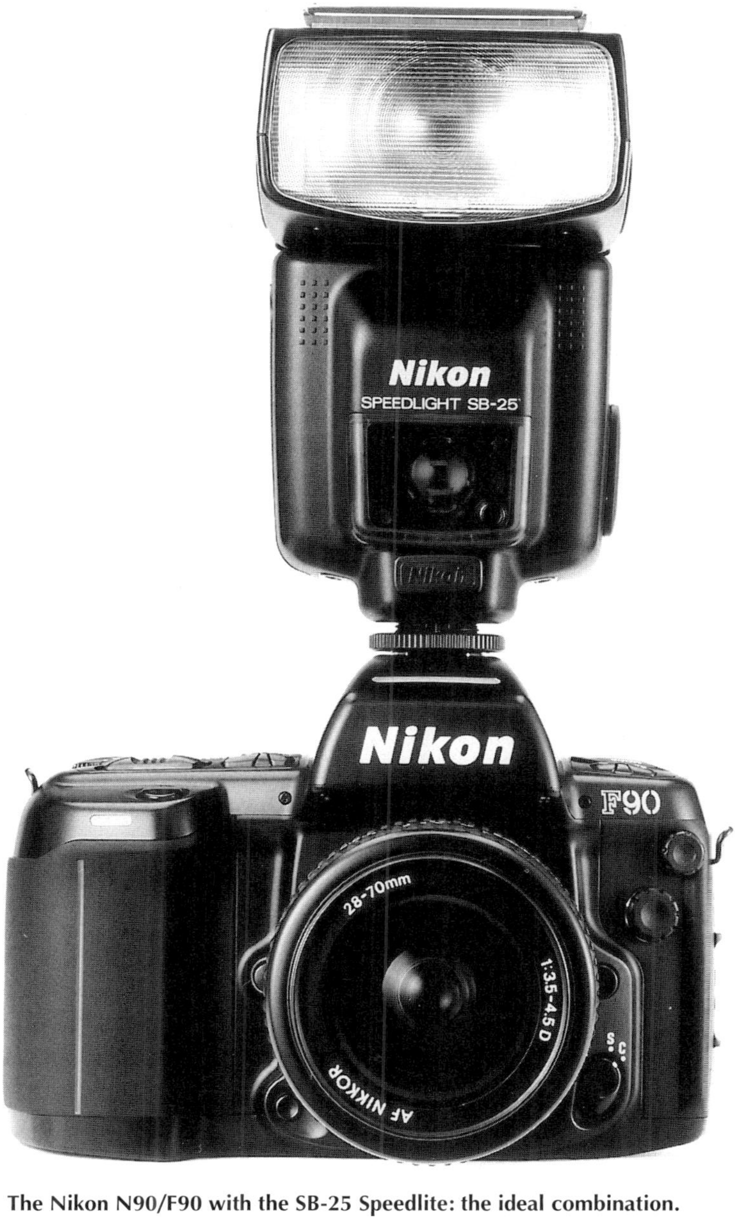

The Nikon N90/F90 with the SB-25 Speedlite: the ideal combination.

The Nikon System flash range.

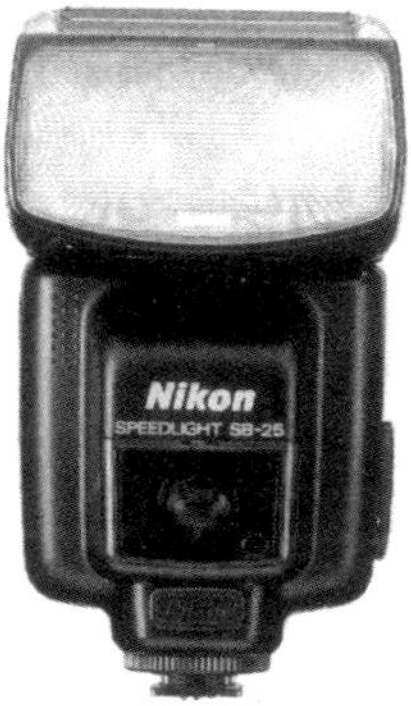

SB-25

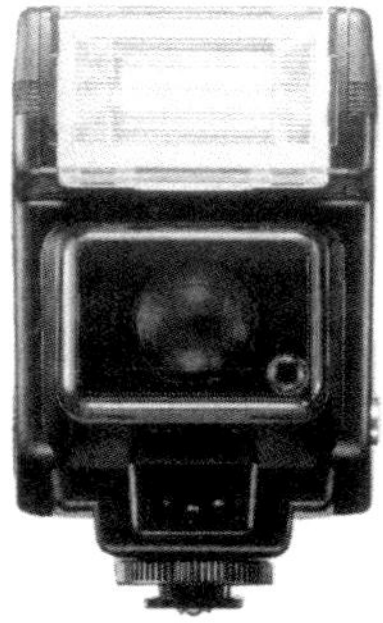

SB-22

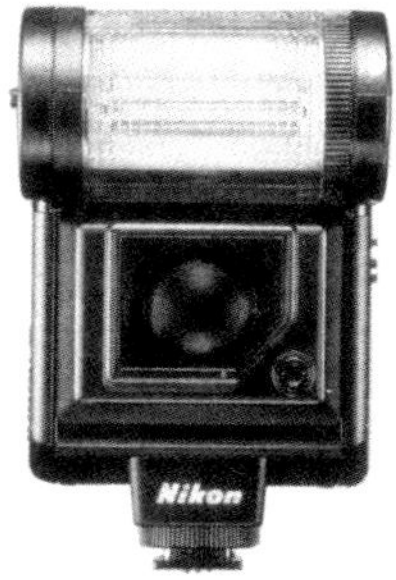

SB-20

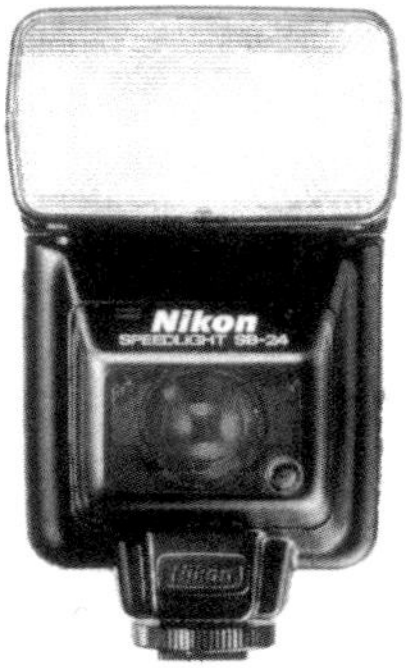

SB-24

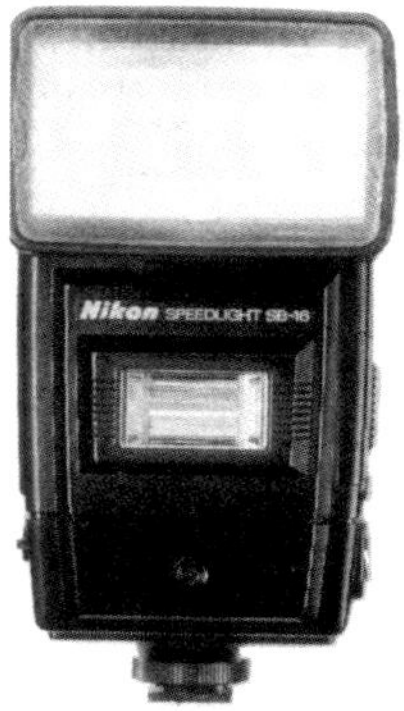

SB-16B

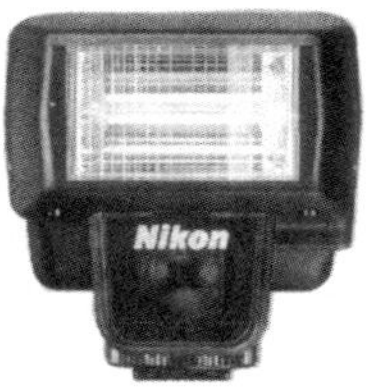

SB-23

Top: With an ISO 400 film, 28mm focal length, and f/8 at 1/60 second, the subject was basically illuminated by the conservatively-used flash in SLOW and REAR modes. Only the cars' lights have motion blurs that appear natural, thanks to REAR mode.

Bottom: Using the stroboscopic setting, the SB-25 was set so that four flashes were triggered during the 1/15 second exposure. Thanks to the black background and total darkness, it was not necessary to change the automatically-selected aperture.

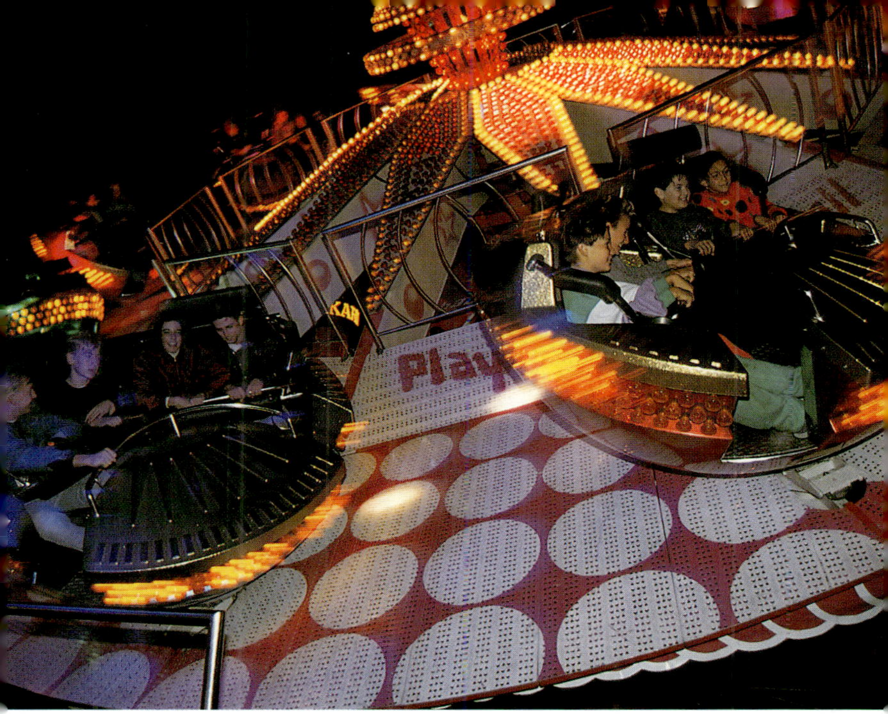
Play

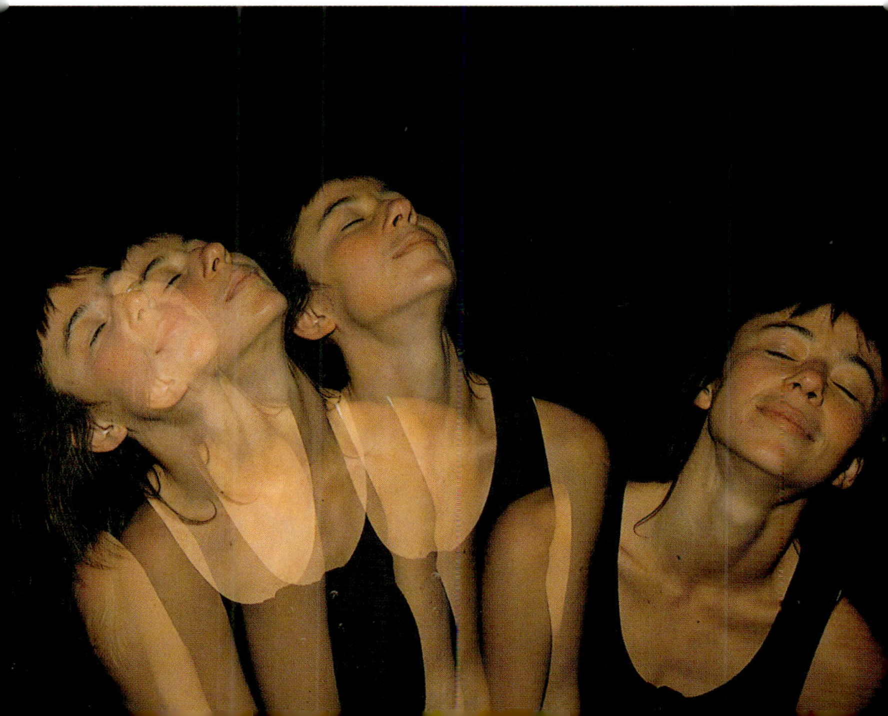

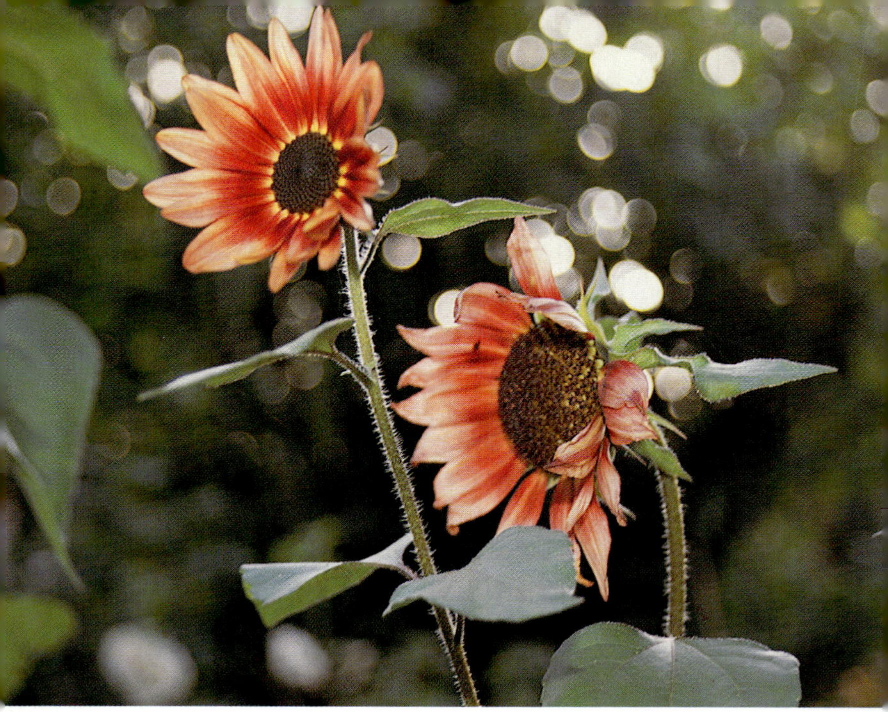

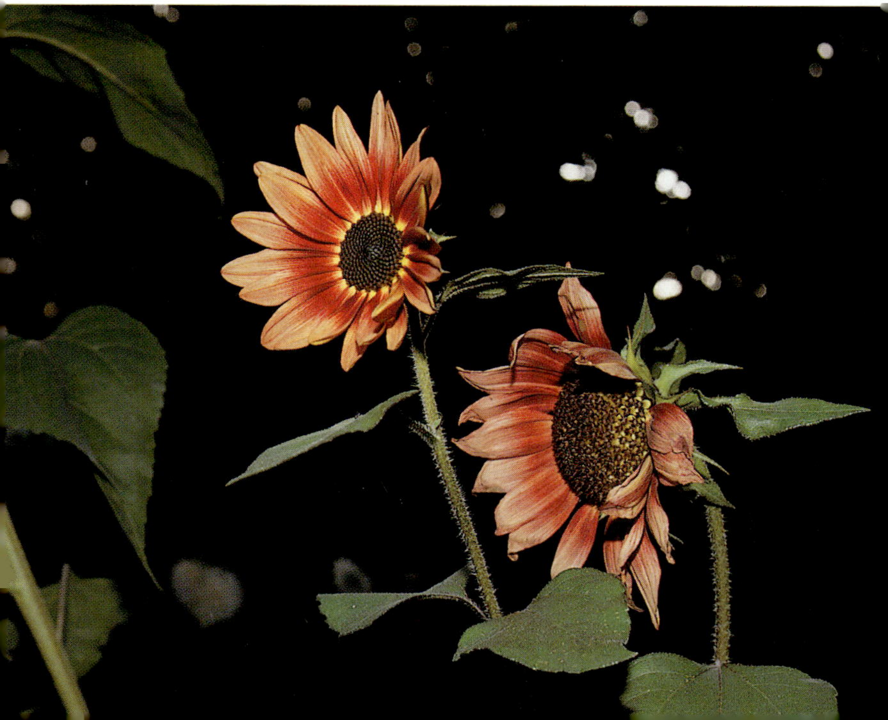

function is seldom used, but is an interesting accessory worth occasional experimentation.

The SB-25's LCD panel can be illuminated and relays relevant information, including the flash mode, minimum and maximum distance coverage, and necessary aperture (in manual modes).

Nikon's external battery packs SD-8 and SD-7 can be connected to the SB-25. These batteries, as well as those from other manufacturers, dramatically shorten recycle times, as well as increase the flash's output capacity.

In addition, there are the functions that can only be used with the N90/F90, such as its preflash for red-eye reduction and test flash to "recognize" the subject.

❐ **Overload warning -** The SB-25 is prone to occasional overloads. When this happens, camera cannot be switched from TTL to M. Switch the camera and flash unit off and remove the flash from the camera. Once it has been reconnected, everything will work normally.

Ranges of Nikon System Flash Units

The effective distances and aperture ranges depend on both the sensitivity of the film and on the focal length of the lens being used. In general, though, greatest range of apertures is available with medium film sensitivity and medium subject distance.

Operation parameters of Nikon TTL Speedlites†

Flash Unit	Aperture Range*	Close Focus Distance*	Maximum Range*
SB-20	f/2-f/22	24in.(60cm) - 106in.(270cm)	59in.(150cm)- 709in.(1800cm)
SB-22	f/2-f/22	24in.(60cm)- 63in.(160cm)	43in.(110cm)- 472in.(1200cm)
SB-24	f/1.4-f/32	24in.(60cm)- 146in.(370cm)	51in.(130cm)- 787in.(2000cm)
SB-25	f/1.4-f/32	24in.(60cm)- 75in.(190cm)	59in.(150cm)- 787in.(2000cm)

†At ISO 100 with a 50mm lens
***These figures are according to my tests**

⇦ **Top: Even illumination of both fore- and background resulted from an f/5.6 aperture and a shutter speed of 1/125 second, selected by the N90/F90's fill-flash and program mode, in conjunction with Matrix metering.**

Bottom: Here, the aperture was manually changed to f/11, resulting in an overly-dark background.

Overview of Nikon System Flash Units

Model No.	Guide Number†	Focal length feet/meters	Batteries	Recycling time (sec.)	No. of flashes (approx.)	Built-in AF-Illuminator	Automatic fill-flash	Monitor Preflash+
SB-16B	105/32	28-85mm manual zoom head	4 AA	11	100	No	Yes	No
SB-20	100/30	28-85mm zoom head	4 AA	6	160	Yes	Yes	No
SB-22	83/25	28-35mm diffuser panel	4 AA	4	200	Yes	Yes	No
SB-23	66/20	35mm	4 AA	2	400	Yes	Yes	No
SB-24	138/42	24-85mm motorized zoom head	4 AA	7	100	Yes	Yes	No
SB-25	138/42	24-85mm motorized zoom head, 20mm diffuser panel	4 AA	7	100	Yes	Yes	Yes

† The guide numbers in this overview table relate to ISO 100 and a focal length of 50mm.

* Only in conjunction with N90/F90 or other newer generation camera.

With higher film sensitivities, the aperture is limited to the smaller ones, and the close focus distance increases.

Slower films result in a shorter range, decreased close focus distance, and the availibility of only the larger apertures. The following table, based on original Nikon data, shows that the aperture range of the SB-25 for closeup photography is larger than any other flash unit.

Non-Nikon Flash Units

Before you use flash units made by other manufacturers, be sure that the voltage across the ISO contacts is not more than 12 volts. Some older units use high-voltages which can damage any camera's electronics, not just the N90/F90. In addition, the flash's ISO contact should not be so thick that there is a danger of pressing on the Nikon System contacts in the hot shoe.

When using flash units with other system contacts, be very sure that the unit is fully compatible with Nikon. Furthermore, Nikon cannot be held responsible for damage that results from the use of non-Nikon flash units.

Connection via SCA Adapter

If you do wish to explore non-Nikon flash alternatives, many companies offer Nikon-compatible flash units that even allow TTL control.

The SCA-300 flash units made by manufacturers like Metz and Osram are Nikon compatible through the use of the SCA-343 adapter.

Some companies, Metz included, offer adapters with AF illuminators (SCA-346). In my tests, these SCA flashes work well. But because of the constant change in camera and flash technology, the adapter market is constantly in flux. If you are not absolutely sure when buying a flash, wait. While it may be a cliché, it really is better to be safe than sorry, especially when your expensive equipment is on the line.

❐ **Connecting several flash units -** The SCA-300 system offers a multi-connector SCA-305A that fits the Nikon SCA-343 or SCA-346 AF adapters. These adapters enable the connection of several Nikon-compatible SCA-300 flashes, but compatibility with the N90/F90 is questionable.

❐ **The new system -** At Photokina 1992, Metz introduced a new

SCA-300 adapter system. It is only logical that today's AF cameras use the system contacts for not only the transmission of analog control voltages, but also for digital data transmission. This new system provides for these advancements. Contact Metz for compatability information.

❒ **Cost and performance -** Many manufacturers provide good alternatives to Nikon flash units but they often require special adapters, and in some cases their compatability is questionable. With a little research, however, you should have no problems.

For example, the Metz 40 MZ-2, with the appropriate SCA-3401 adapter, is very similar in function to the SB-25. However, the compatibility with the N90/F90 was still in process when this book went to press.

❒ **Non-dedicated auto-flash -** If your non-Nikon flash unit's compatability is confirmed, here are a few tips for using it with the N90/F90.

Mount the flash onto the camera, select a shutter speed in exposure mode "M" between 1/60 second and 1/250 second, find the appropriate aperture as shown on the back of the flash, and set it on the lens. Check to see if the subject is within the flash range (either on the unit itself or in the instruction manual), and if it is, release the shutter. The flash unit will automatically measure the light reflected from the subject and control the flash duration accordingly. Normally, you will find that even non-dedicated auto-flash takes good pictures.

Operation of simple, manual flash units is much the same as that described except that the focus distance corresponding to the aperture must be strictly adhered to.

When the observer sees these images of street scenes in Algarve (top) and Apulia (bottom), he or she will vicariously enjoy the relaxed lifestyle they portray. ➪

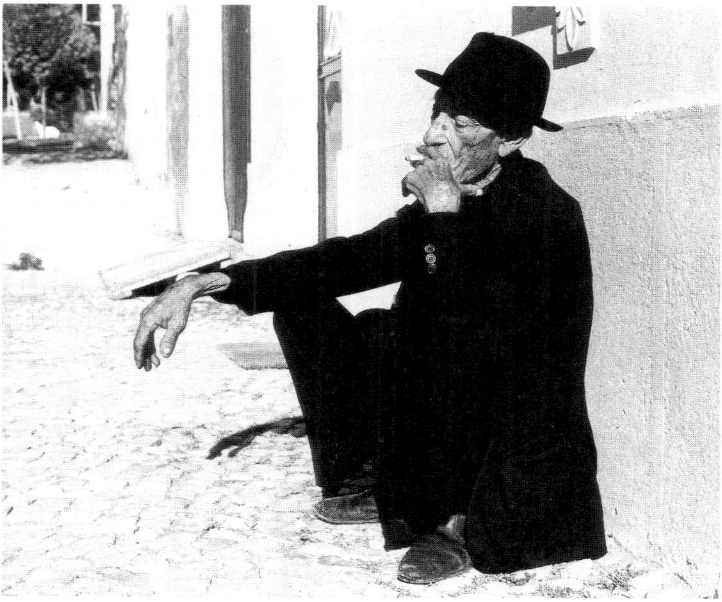

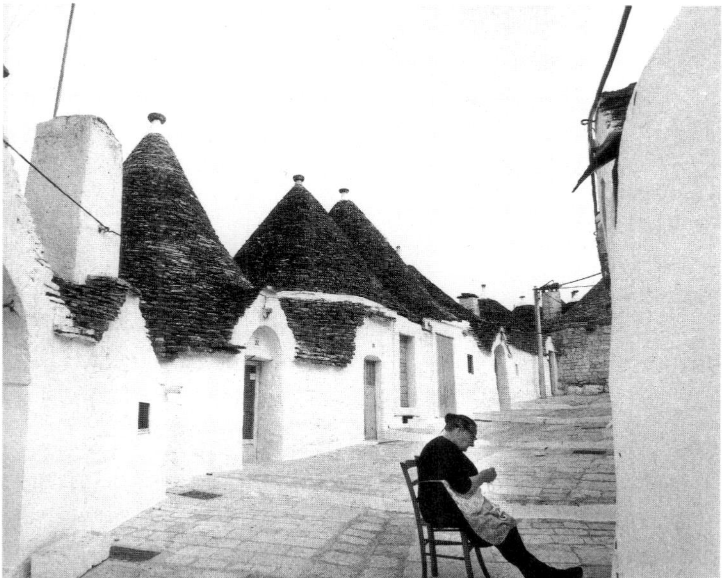

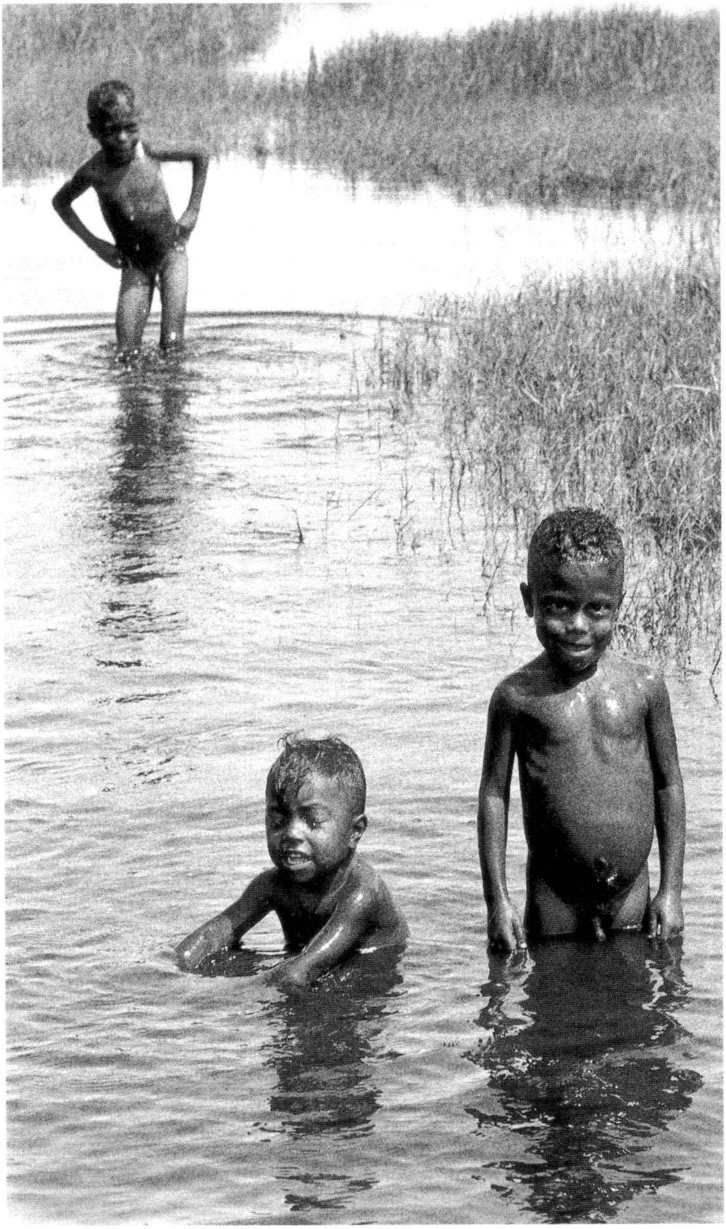

Lenses

Compatible Lenses

The lens table at the end of this book gives an overview of all of the AF-, AF-I, and type D AF Nikkors that can be used with the N90/F90.

Be advised, however, that certain non-AI Nikkor, fisheye, AI telezooms and telephoto, and older PC Nikkor lenses are incompatible with the N90/F90. Furthermore, older Reflex Nikkors and the Nikon F3AF's AF lenses and converters should not be used. If in doubt, check with Nikon for details.

While the newer lenses described at the end of the book take advantage of all of the N90/F90's features, the majority of older AI Nikkors, only work with the N90/F90's "A" and "M" modes, and with center-weighted or spot metering. If in doubt, find a copy of the actual Nikon lens literature. If necessary, request it directly from Nikon.

This picture of children in Brazil is an attempt at objective reporting.

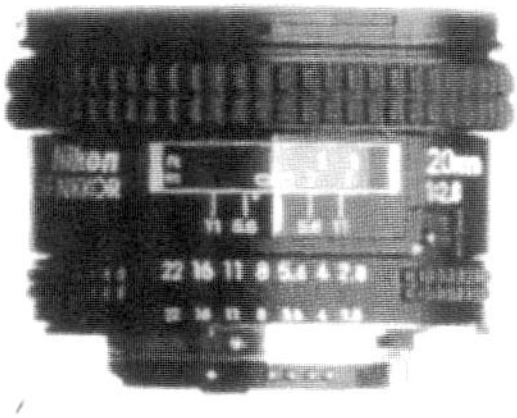

20 mm f/2.8

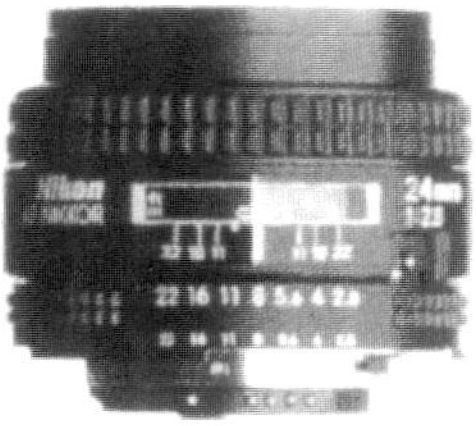

24 mm f/2.8

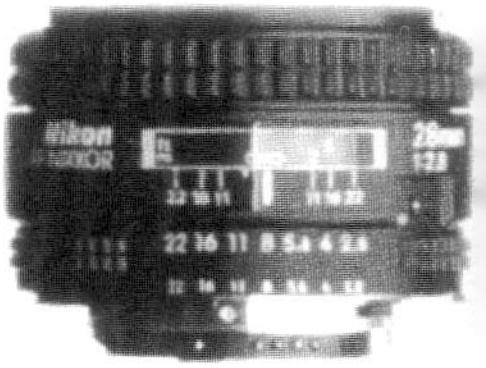

28 mm f/2.8

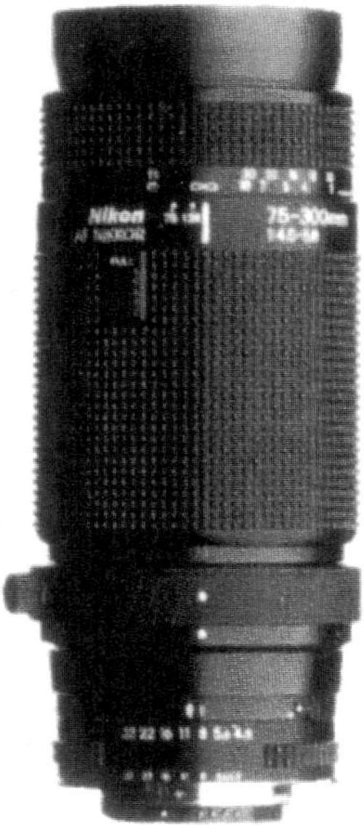

75-300 mm f/4.5-5.6

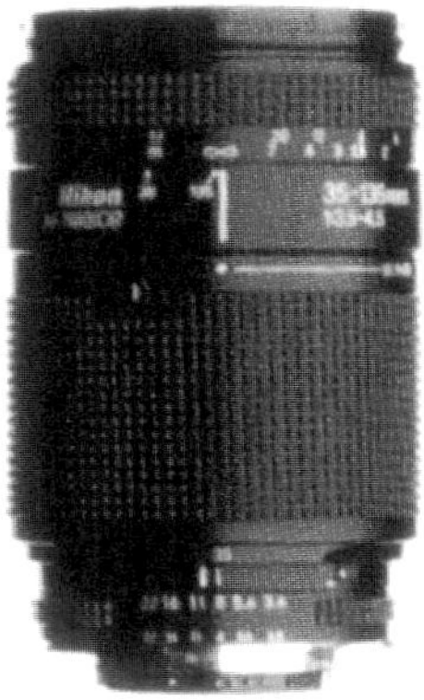

35-135 mm f/3.5-4.5

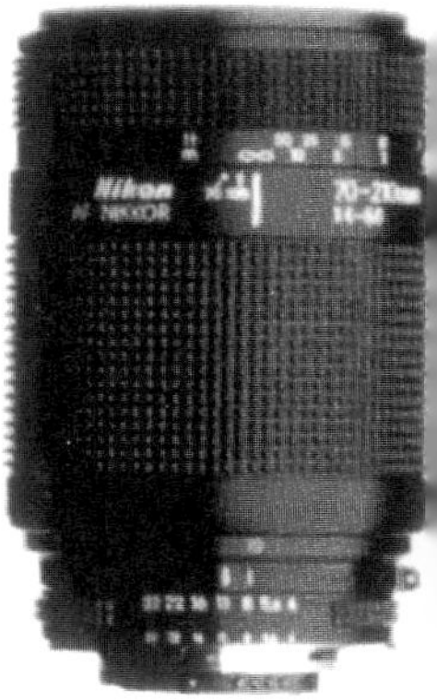

70-210 mm f/4.0-5.6

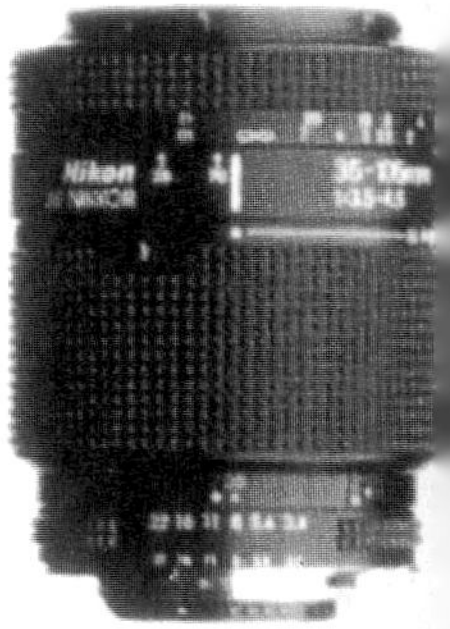

35-105 mm f/3.5-4.5

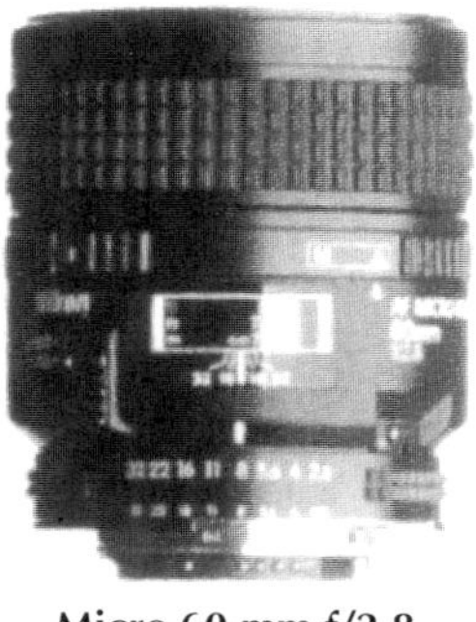

Micro 60 mm f/2.8

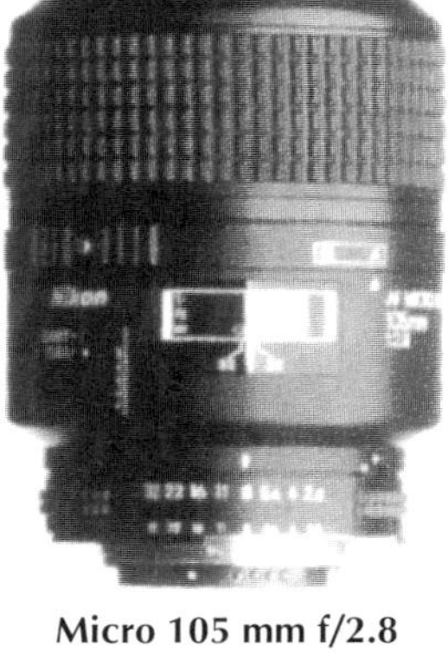

Micro 105 mm f/2.8

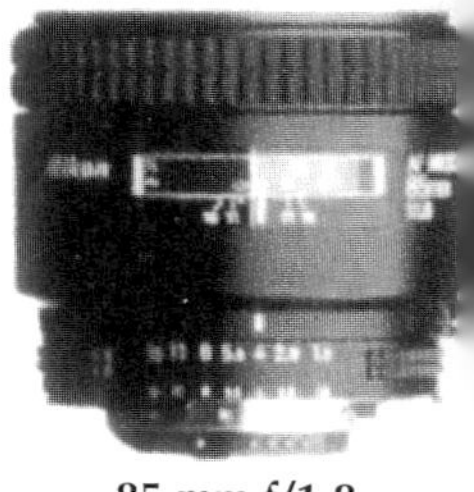

85 mm f/1.8

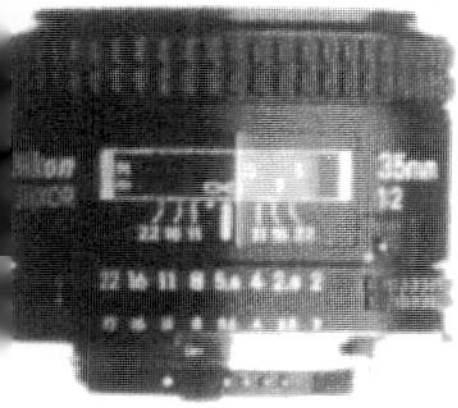

35 mm f/2.0

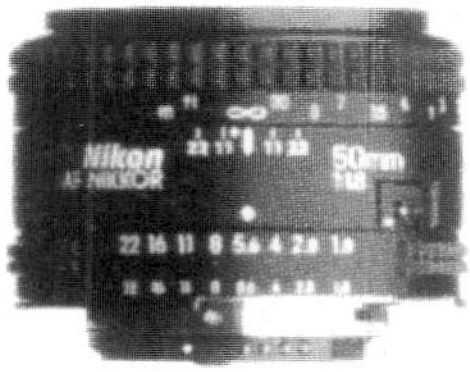

50 mm f/1.4

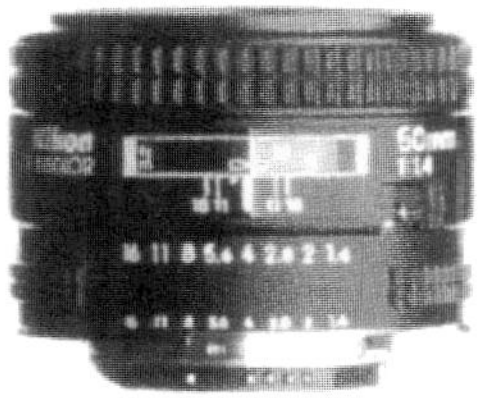

50 mm f/1.8

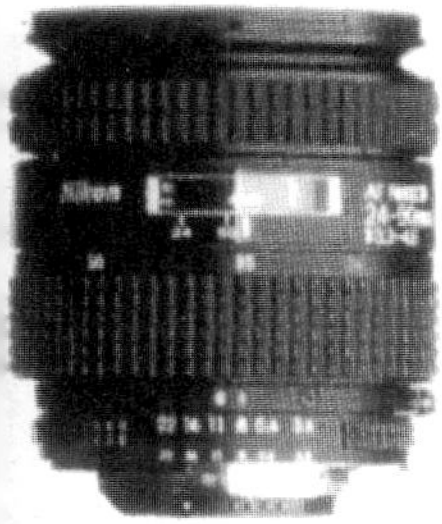

24-50 mm f/3.3-4.5

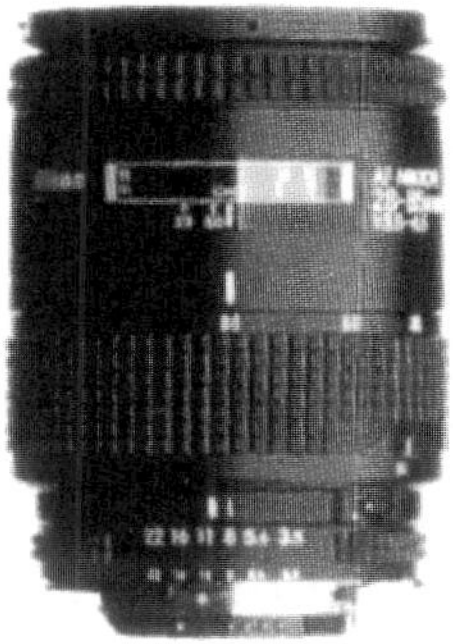

28-85 mm f/3.5-4.5

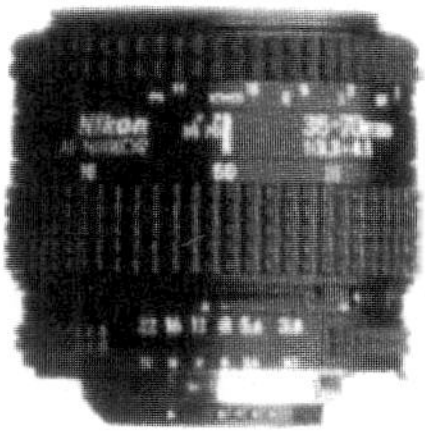

35-70 mm f/3.3-4.5

An overview of conventional AF Nikkors

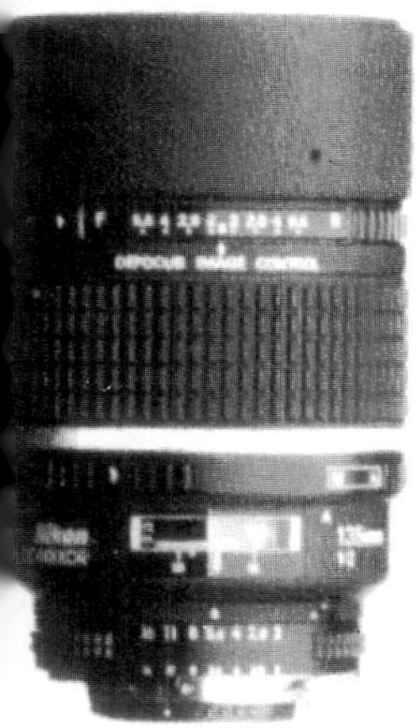

135 mm f/2.0 DC

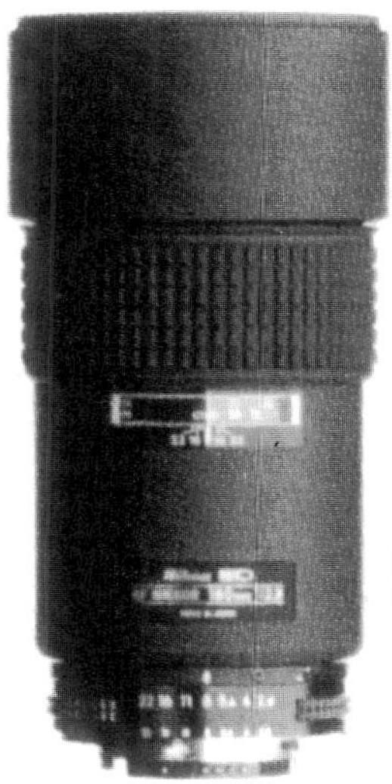

180 mm f/2.8 IF-ED

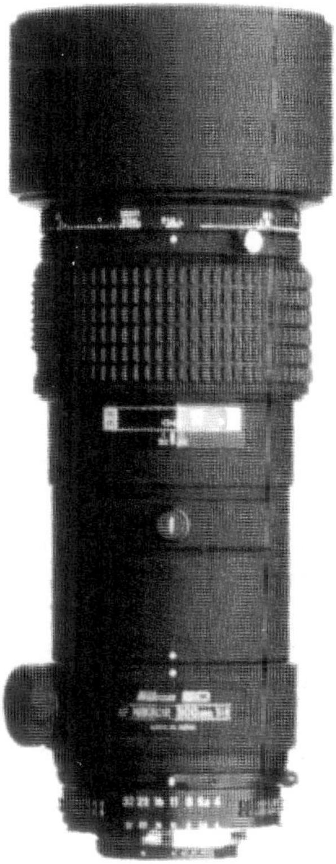

300 mm f/4.0 IF-ED

A Tour of Nikkor Lenses

Nikon is respected as the manufacturer of some of the finest quality lenses available today. Here is a brief overview of some of the most popular.

❒ **Extreme wide-angle and fisheye -** Fisheyes are used in very specialized situations because of their uncorrected spherical

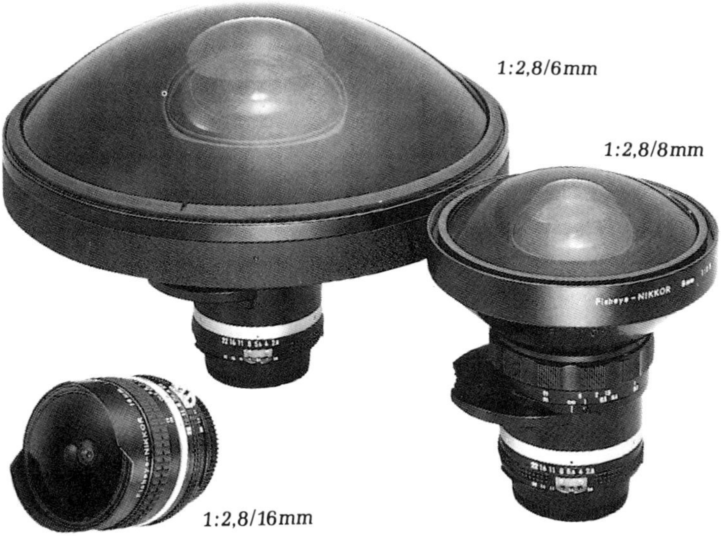

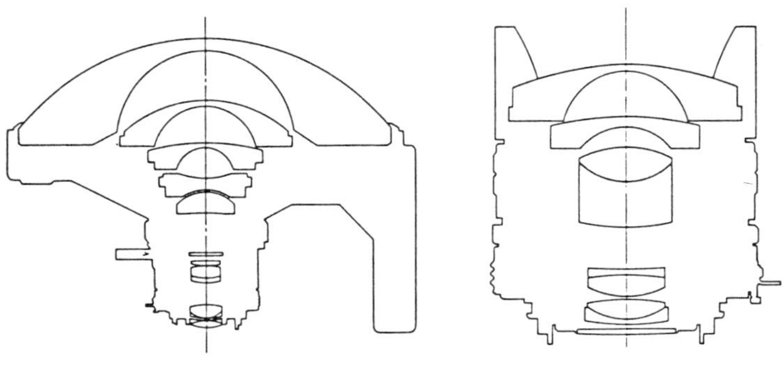

These cross-sections show the internal differences between a super-fisheye lens and the rectilinear-perspective 16mm.

distortion. For occasional special effects, the 6mm f/2.8 is an interesting (and incredibly expensive) toy to have, but for everyday photography it is all but useless. Who needs 220° picture coverage anyway? The AF fisheye type D 16mm f/2.8 is a lower-priced and less hefty alternative.

Alternatives with normal, rectilinear perspectives include the 13mm f/5.6 (118°) and the 15mm f/3.5 (110°) Nikkors.

❒ **Wide-angle -** The AF 20mm f/2.8 is recommended for landscape, close-quarter, and even architectural photography. I have been using this lens for quite a while, and am very pleased with the results.

A less extreme option for these applications is the AF 24mm f/2.8 or the new type D AF 28mm f/1.4. Additionally, the bright AF 35mm f/2.0 is an excellent lens and has proven its worth in my work.

❒ **Wide-angle zoom -** Two versatile choices in this catagory are the AF 24-50mm f/3.3-4.5 and the type D AF 20-35mm f/2.8. Both are good because they have broader applications than just straightforward wide-angle photography.

❒ **Normal fixed-focus -** If you were to select a single "normal" AF Nikkor, the 50mm f/1.4 would probably be your first choice. It offers outstanding optical quality together with fast speed.

For macro fans, the AF Micro-Nikkor 60mm f/2.8 is an excellent, albeit expensive, choice. This lens offers a macro ratio of 1:1 without any accessories.

❒ **Normal zoom -** The top of this list includes the type D AF 28-70mm f/3.5-4.5 and the type D AF 35-70mm f/2.8. Less expensive alternatives include the AF 28-85mm f/3.5-4.5, the AF 35-105mm f/3.5-4.5, and the AF 35-135mm f/3.5-4.5. With today's zooms, there is really no reason to worry about quality; they are absolutely first-rate.

❒ **Short to medium zoom -** The economical AF 70-210mm f/4.0-5.6 is an alternative to expensive fixed focal length lenses.

The AF 80-200mm ED f/2.8 is expensive, but also of incredible quality. It is mechanically solid, offers exceptionally smooth manual focusing, but is rather cumbersome and heavy. It is now also available in a redesigned type D version, perfect for the N90/F90.

❒ **Tele-zoom -** The AF 75-300mm f/4.5-5.6 offers a wide focal range in a relatively compact package. It is particularly useful in sport or news photography where you need to be able to react quickly to large differences in subject distance.

❒ **Short telephoto -** The AF 85mm f/1.8 is a relatively economical AF fixed focal Nikon lens that leaves nothing to be desired. Thanks to its fast speed, this lens enables shots where the subject is in focus and in front of a soft background.

The expensive AF Micro Nikkor 105mm f/2.8 is an excellent lens that takes not only macro shots (stepless magnification ratio up to 1:1) but also normal portraits.

New from Nikon is the AF DC 105mm f/2.0 portrait lens with variable soft focus effects.

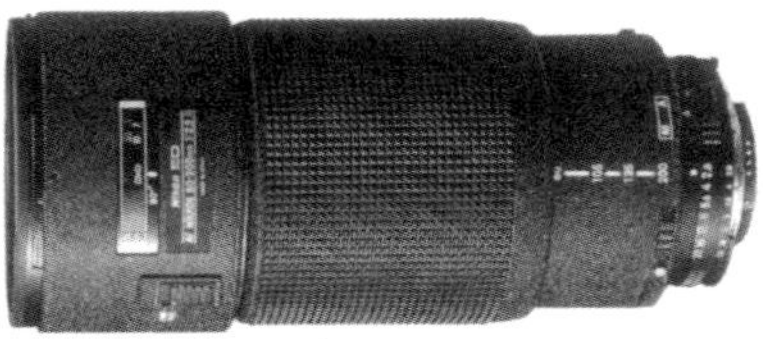

AF 1:2,8/200 mm D ED

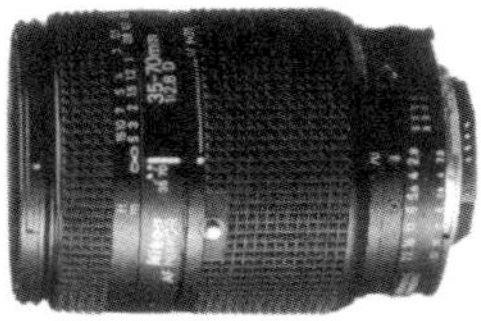

AF 1:2,8/35-70 mm D

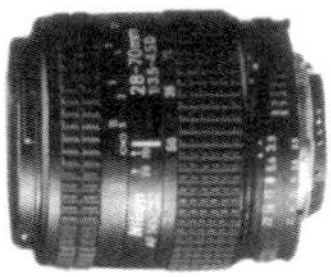

AF 1:3,5-4,5/28-70 mm D

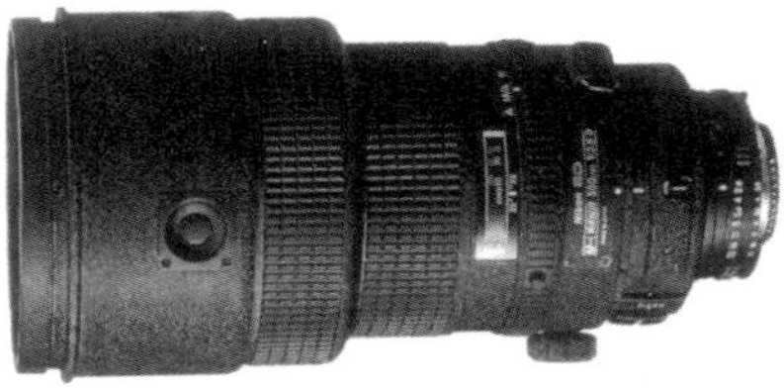

AF-I 1:2,8/300 mm D IF-ED

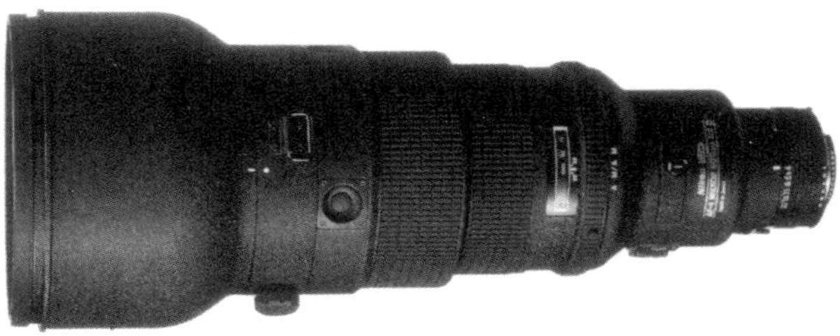

AF-I 1:4/600 mm D IF-ED

An overview of AF and AF-I Nikkors.

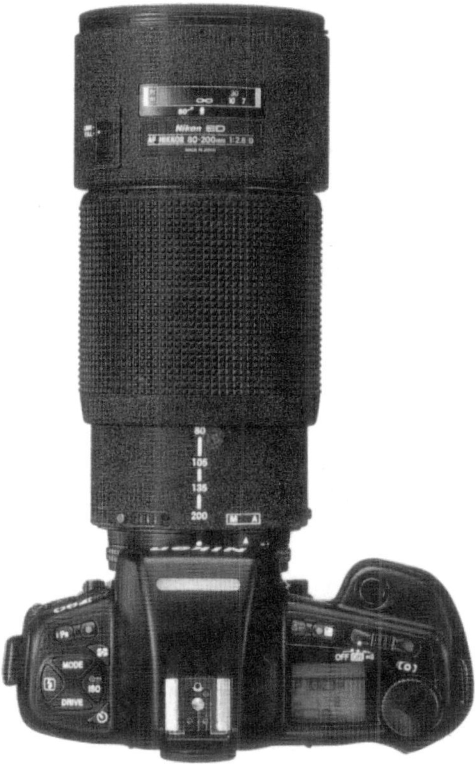

The 80-200mm f/2.8 D ED is perhaps the best telephoto zoom lens available for the N90/F90.

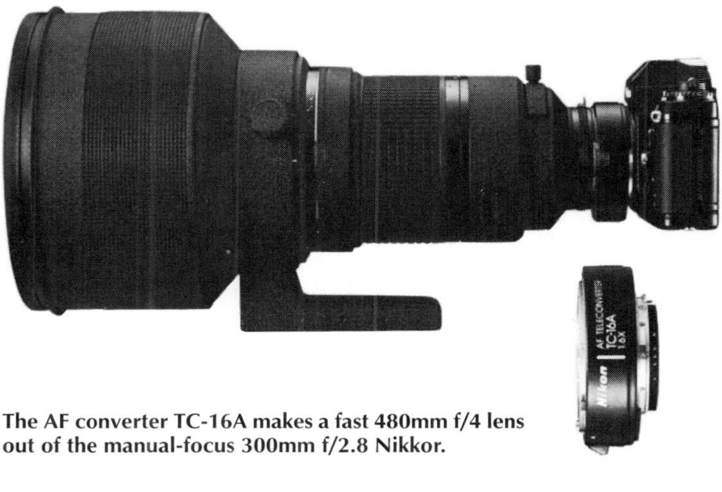

The AF converter TC-16A makes a fast 480mm f/4 lens out of the manual-focus 300mm f/2.8 Nikkor.

❒ **Medium telephoto -** Nikon's AF 180mm f/2.8 IF-ED is a lens that, thanks to an internal focusing mechanism, can not only be focused very quickly by the autofocus system, but also has particularly high optical quality thanks to the use of special element-reducing glass.

❒ **Super telephoto -** Nikon has a truly super lens in the AF 300mm f/2.8 IF-ED. It is the large, expensive lens that you see on the television being used by photojournalists and sports photographers. Now available as the redesigned type D AF-I 300mm f/2.8 IF-ED. Thanks to its particularly powerful, built-in focusing motor, this lens is a true stunner, especially when used with the N90/F90. Unfortunately, its stratospheric price tag puts it out of the reach of most photographers.

A lighter, more compact, and less expensive alternative is the 300mm f/4.0 IF-ED. While it is not as fast as the f/2.8 lens, its optical quality is just as good.

Should you need an even longer focal length, the new type D AF-I 400mm f/2.8 and the acclaimed 500mm f/4.0 IF-ED are available. The latter has a built-in RAM chip and is fully compatible with all of the N90/F90's modes (except autofocus). The last word in super-telephoto lenses is, by the way, the fully N90/F90 compatible type D AF-I 600mm f/4.0 IF-ED.

❒ **Shift -** These lenses are used in architecture photography. Their optics actually "shift" to avoid converging lines, making the images

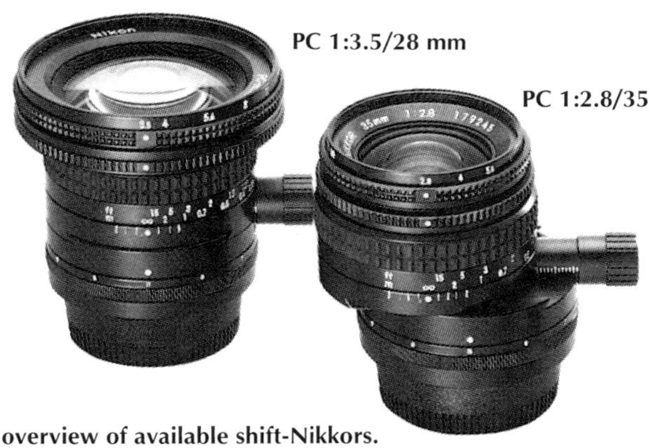

An overview of available shift-Nikkors.

look more realistic. When using a shift lens, you can shoot from a low angle and from a relatively close distance without worrying about distortion.

Such complicated optics are obviously not compatible with the N90/F90's autofocusing systems. You can use the PC 28mm f/3.5 and PC 35mm f/2.8 in "M" or "A" modes, with center-weighted or spot metering. If you plan to invest in one of these specialized lenses, I recommend buying the 28mm, simply because in many instances the 35mm's perspective is just not wide enough.

Non-Nikkor Lenses

As we have seen, Nikon has a particularly good range of AF lenses available. You may, however, wish to explore the options offerd by other companies. It is important to note, however, that while Nikon guarantees flawless performance of its lenses with the N90/F90, no such guarantee covers lenses made by other manufacturers. If you purchase a Nikon-compatible lens from a reputable manufacturer (I consider Tamron, Tokina and Sigma to be reputable), the risk is not very high. These firms have been in the photographic industry for many years, and, as I can attest to from personal experience, offer reliable and fairly quick warranty repairs.

❐ **Range** - Both Tamron and Sigma offer a wide range of Nikon-compatible autofocus lenses. Sigma has a 28-70mm f/3.5-4.5, a fast 75-200mm f/3.8, and a particularly brilliant 70-210mm f/3.5-4.5 APO. Their fixed focal length 24mm f/2.8 and Macro 90mm f/2.8 (stepless to 1:2, using the included closeup filter, 1:1) are worth considering. A runner-up is the relatively economical 400mm f/5.6.

Tamron offers a 35-90mm f/4-5.6, a 90-300mm f/4.5-5.6, an ultra-compact 28-200 f/3.8-5.6, a continuous-focus macro 90mm f/2.5, a 35-105mm f/2.8 constant aperture, a 70-210mm f/2.8, and a 300mm f/2.8. These lenses are all especially lightweight.

Selecting the Right Lens

With the vast array of lenses available, it is entirely possible that you are confused about which lens is right for you. The main decision you will have to make is whether to purchase several fixed-focal length lenses or a zoom. Everyone knows the merits of the former; let's look at the advantages and disadvantages of zoom lenses.

Zooms

When using zoom lenses, there are several inherent advantages. You do not need to change lenses as often, so shooting is faster and more flexible. Additionally, you have fewer lenses to drag along and those that you buy are cheaper than the sum of the corresponding fixed focal length lenses.

Unfortunately, zooms are often so heavy and bulky that you will want to leave them at home anyway. Happily, though, these lenses are becoming more and more compact and lightweight.

❒ **Mass and volume -** Let's compare, for example, a few AF Nikkor lenses in the 70mm to 210mm range. The fixed AF 85mm f/1.8 has 6 elements, weighs 14.6 ounces (415g) and is 2.3 inches (5.8cm) long. The AF 180mm f/2.8 IF-ED has 8 elements, weighs 26 ounces (750g) and is 5.7 inches (14.4cm) long.

The comparable AF 70-210mm f/4.0-5.6 is only half as heavy but some find it difficult to handle. With respect to speed and optical quality (12 elements), the zoom is somewhat slower and may lose a little in optical quality.

The AF 80-200mm f/2.8 ED is excellent, but more expensive. And even though the speed is good and the optical quality is excellent, its weight of 42 ounces (1200g) and length make it fairly bulky.

❒ **Price and quality -** Good zoom lenses usually cost decidedly less than the sum of fixed focals. But whether or not this equals a "good value" depends on the lens' quality. A zoom that equals the quality of fixed focals is an expensive piece of equipment.

Sharp zooms result from special glass, element shape, floating elements, very precise mechanics, and other costly ingredients. And to keep internal flare and dispersion to a minimum, the technical intricacies become immense. The end result are lenses that, while convenient and of superb quality, are frightfully expensive.

To keep cost down, zooms are often made slower than their fixed length counterparts. The trend towards lighter, brighter, and more compact zooms sometimes equals a step back in optical quality. When buying a lens, buy the one that does the job with the least elements; it could very well create brilliant pictures in critical cases. And unless you are copying slides, some limited distortion should not really matter.

❐ **The Verdict -** Every zoom lens is a compromise between focal range, performance speed, weight, size, and cost. Since contemporary zooms these days are being made in larger batches than traditional fixed focals, the manufacturers have more than compensated for the price disadvantage. Whether or not this

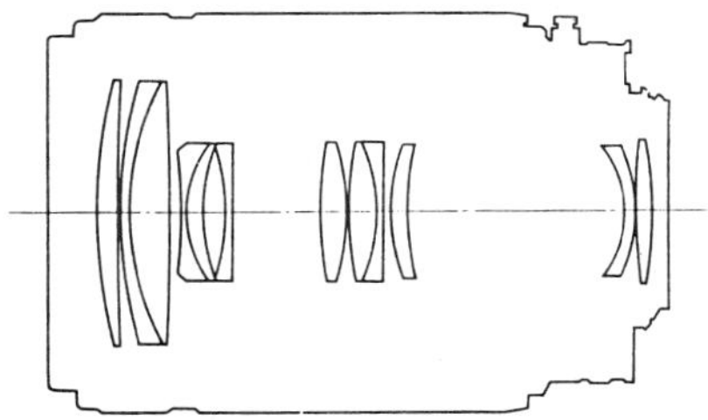

AF 4.0-5.6/70-210 mm

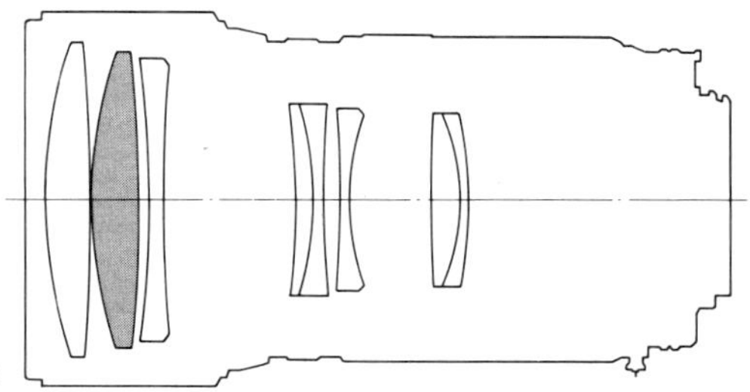

AF 2.8/180 mm IF-ED

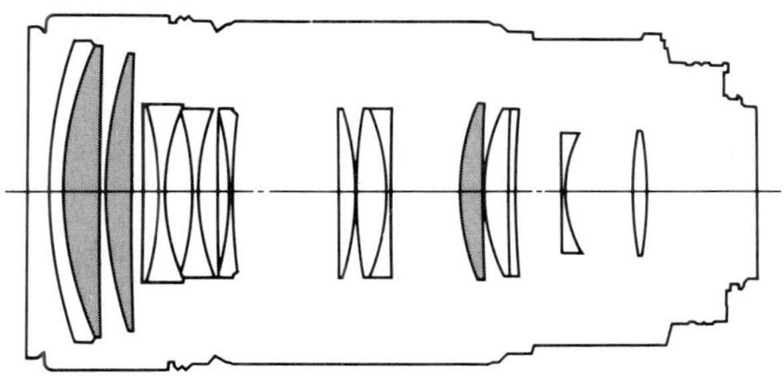

AF 2.8/80-200 mm ED

A Comparison of zooms and fixed focal lengths.

savings is passed on to the consumer or if it is reinvested in research and development, nobody knows. The bottom line is that you get what you pay for. Some zooms are of higher optical caliber than fixed-focus lenses, and some are not. One thing is for sure: they are only getting better.

What to Buy

"Light, short, fast, brilliant, super sharp, 28-300mm zoom range..." this is how many photographers would describe the perfect lens. Finding this lens is just about as likely as finding a beautiful, quiet apartment downtown, in the middle of a park, for $300 a month.

However, in shopping for a lens, you will probably discover that you actually are willing to drag a few more ounces and inches through the countryside, as well as to pay a few more dollars in order to have the lens that will truly serve your needs.

It should be noted that as of the time of writing, no independent lens manufacurer offers a lens with distance transmitting (type D) capability, and for this reason none of them will work with the N90/F90's 3D Matrix metering or 3D flash capabilities.

The Verdict

My recommendation is to purchase your N90/F90 with the type D AF Nikkor 28-70mm f/3.5-4.5 instead of the 50mm f/1.8. It has proven itself to be a very capable "normal" lens. It can be joined by the AF Nikkor 20mm f/2.8 for landscape work and with the type D AF Nikkor 80-200mm f/2.8 for action. With these three lenses, you will be prepared for any situation. If you often shoot portraits, you should consider the AF 85mm f/1.8, the AF Micro Nikkor 105 f/2.8 or the type D AF DC 105mm f/2.0.

Those of you who regularly shoot sports or news photos either professionally or semi-professionally will probably not be able to get along without one of the new AF-I Nikkors.

Lens and Autofocusing Accessories

There is a wide range of accessories available from Nikon, each designed to enhance the performance of your N90/F90. Here are just a few of them.

An Overview of close-up accessories

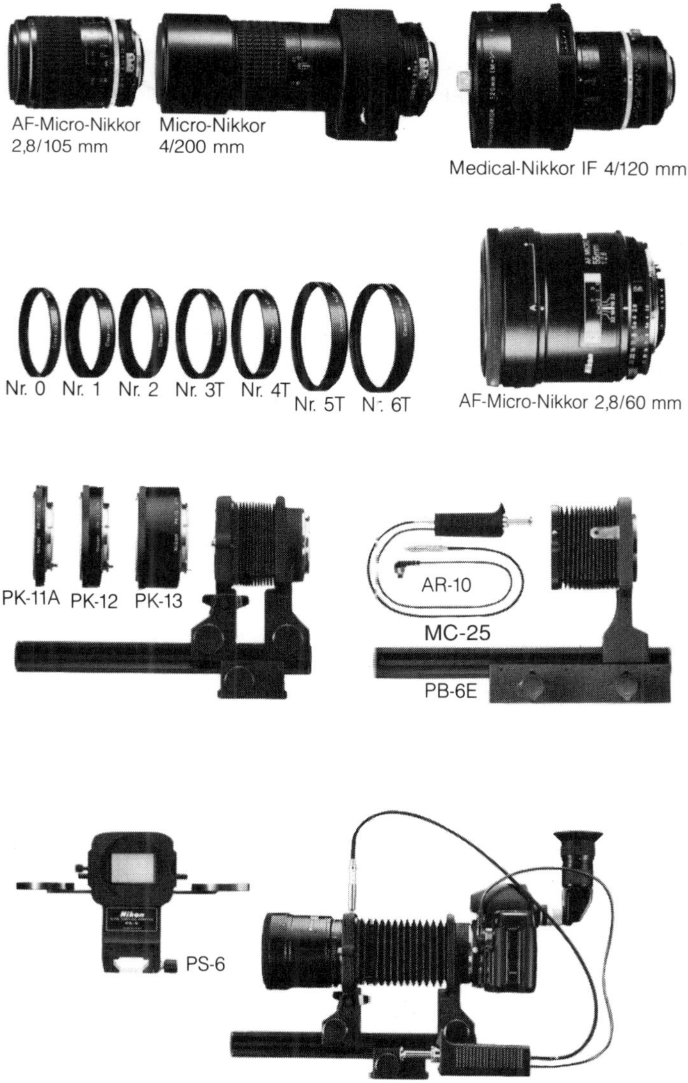

AF- and Tele-converters

Tele-converters fit between the camera body and lens and effectively increase the focal length of the lens. For example, Nikon's most popular model, the TC-16A, increases the focal length by a facor of 1.6x; a 200mm lens, used with the TC-16A, becomes a 320mm. The downsides are that the effective maximum aperture becomes smaller, and the image quality of a lens with a converter is always a bit lower than the same lens without one. Nevertheless, for most applications, the image quality produced with a tele-converter is perfectly acceptable. Compatability with the N90/F90 should be no problem.

Nikon's recently introduced AF-I tele-converters are designed to allow Nikon autofocusing systems to control non-autofocus lenses. What they really have to offer; we will have to wait and see.

Macro Accessories

According to most textbooks, only pictures with a magnification ratio of 1:1 or higher are truly macro. Normally, however, the accepted definition includes ratios to 1:4.

❒ **Extension tubes -** The only extension tube that is compatible with the N90/F90 is the PZ-11A. The PK-11 is not, so be very careful when purchasing. Extension tubes do their job, but I personally prefer the alternative macro lenses or close-up lenses; they are easier to use and more flexible.

❒ **Close-up lenses -** Close-up lenses (sometimes called diopters) are the least expensive macro photography option. When screwed into the lens's filter thread, they shorten the minimum focusing distance. You can, therefore, get closer to your subject and increase the magnification ratio. You can even get a ratio up to 1:1, depending on the lens and the filter. Nikon makes closeup lenses with +0.7, +1.5 and +3 diopter in the 52mm filter size. I particularly recommend the achromatic closeup lenses, which Nikon offers in +1.5 and +2.9 diopters in both 52mm and 62mm sizes.

Top: Aletsch, the longest glacier in Europe is a frame-filling image for a fish-eye lens. To obtain an ideal exposure for both snow and sky, a manual exposure correction on the grey rocks was used. ➪

Bottom: The twilight scene in Montreaux on Lake Geneva was captured particularly well with a 24mm lens and Matrix metering.

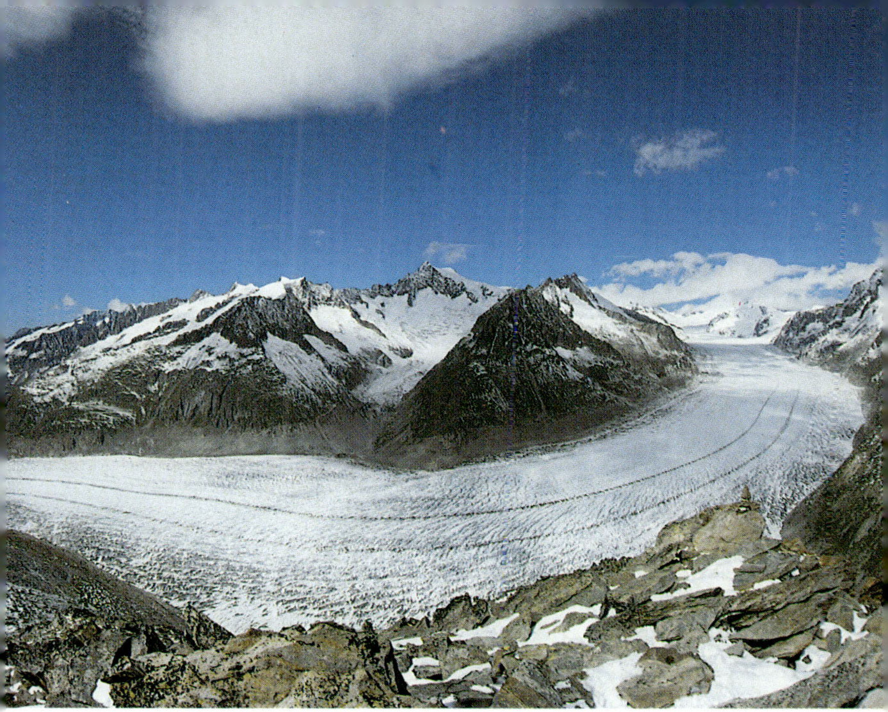

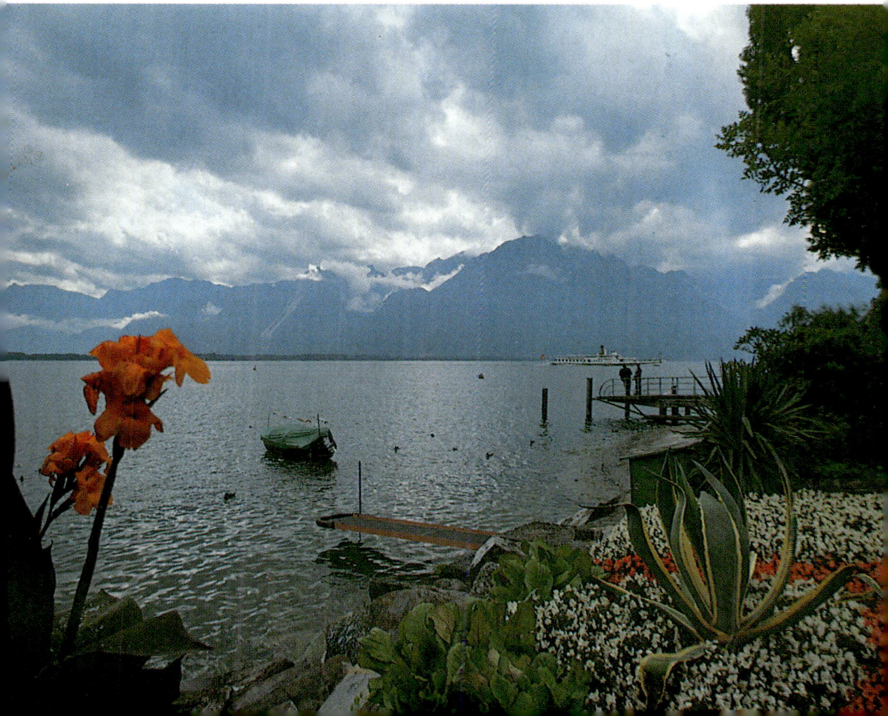

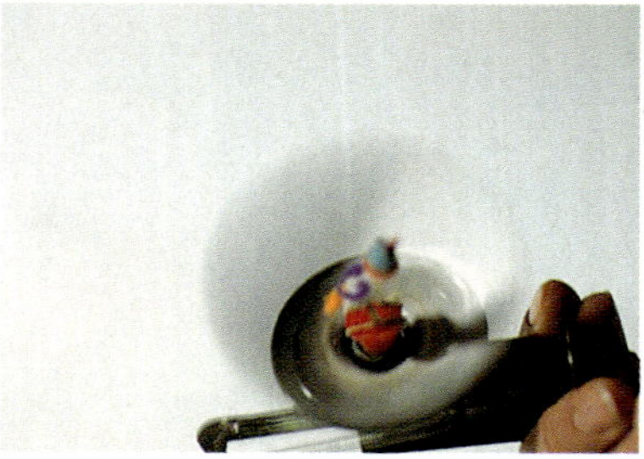

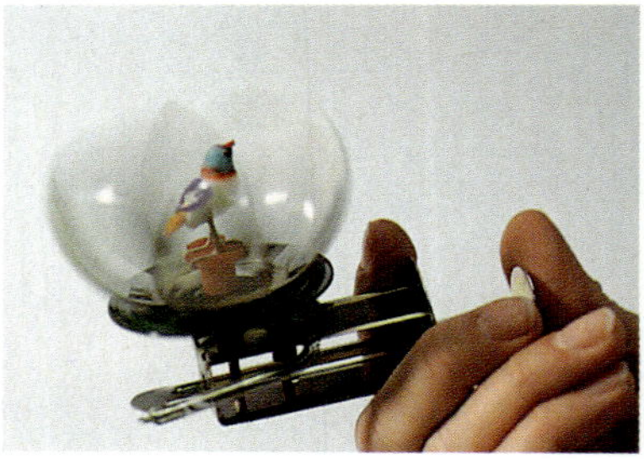

a

b

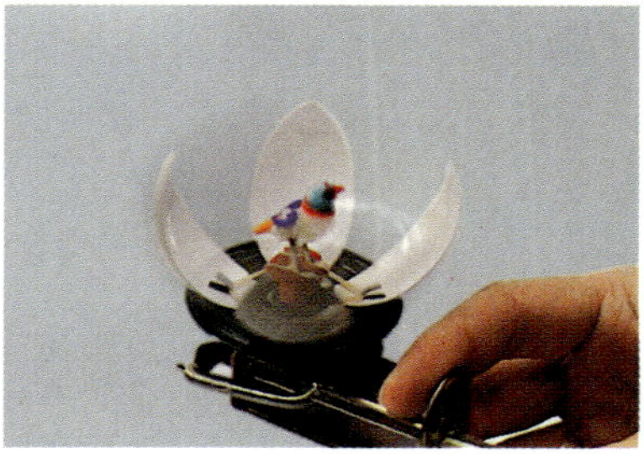

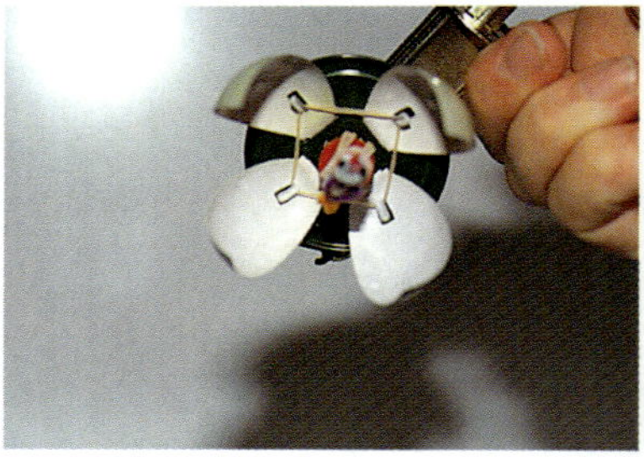

c

d

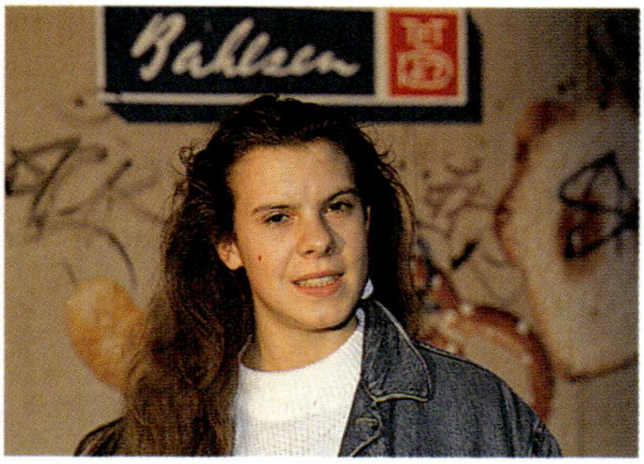

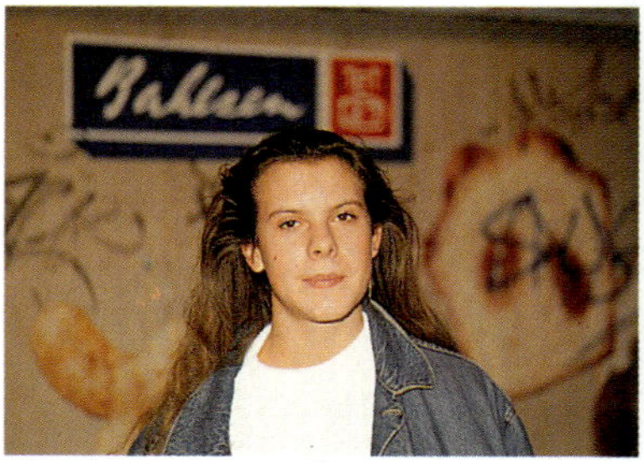

e

f

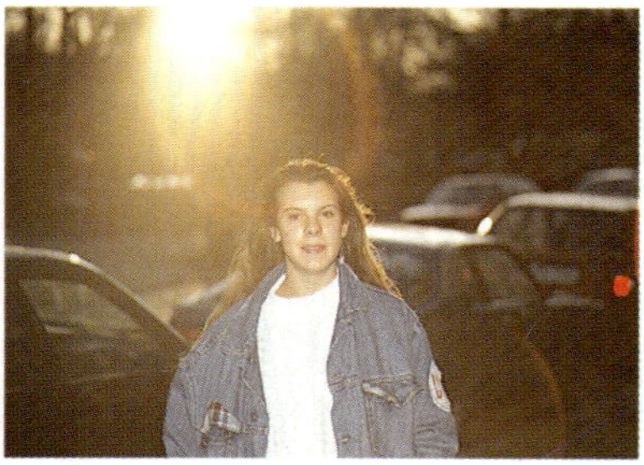

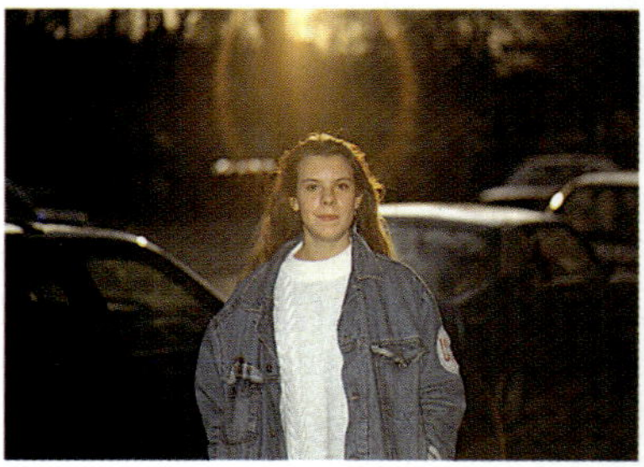

g

h

When using closeup lenses, indeed as with all macro photography, you should stop down as much as possible. In this manner you can compensate for the natural reduction in quality the use of closeup lenses creates. Besides, depth of field is so minimal in macro photography that stopping down can only improve the quality of the entire image.

❒ **Autofocus close-ups -** In my tests, I found that AF Nikkors are well suited to macro photography, even with close-up diopters attached. The autofocus system only works, however, if you are within the distance to the subject in which focusing is actually possible. In other words, the autofocus only works with closeup lenses if you could have focused just as well manually. My tip is to try focusing manually first to determine the distance, and then switch to AF mode.

❒ **Micro lenses -** Nikon calls their macro Nikkor lenses "Micro." These lenses, unlike their standard equivalents, are also corrected to work perfectly in the normal, non-macro range. "Floating elements" enable these lenses to change steplessly from infinity to macro, depending on the distance setting. Nikon offers two such lenses at this time: the AF Micro 105mm f/2.8 and the AF Micro 60mm f/2.8. The latter is optically superb, offering a focal range from infinity to 9 inches (23cm), corresponding to 1:1. Since it can also be used perfectly in normal shooting, it is an ideal macro lens to own.

The same is true for the AF Micro 105mm f/2.8 that allows portraits or 1:1 macro, steplessly. Additionally, this longer focal length increases the distance between subject and lens, reducing problems of small animals running away, and problems with shadows when using flash. Both of AF Micros have a nice, wide manual focusing ring and focus just as easily as conventional lenses.

⇦ **FP mode allows extremely short flash sync times (even 1/4000 second). Fast-moving objects can thus be completely frozen even with strong ambient light; back-lit subjects can be separated when using large apertures:**

a) Shot at f/4 at 1/60 without flash, the motion is completely blurred.
b) Shot at f/4 at 1/60 with "normal" TTL fill-flash, a sharp flash image has an unsharp ambient light image overlaid on it.
c) manual exposure in FP mode at f/5.6 at 1/2000.
d) The motion is completely frozen at f/4 at 1/4000.
e) + g) No flash.
f) + h) Flash in FP mode.

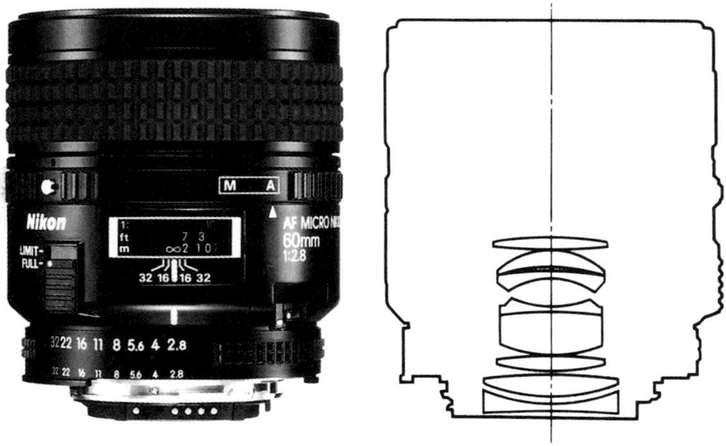

AF-Micro-Nikkor 2.8/60mm

In the manual focus sector, both the Micro 105mm f/2.8, Micro 200mm f/4, and the medical 120mm f/4 are compatible with the N90/F90 in "M" and "A" modes and with center-weighted metering. The medical Nikkor has a built-in ring flash whose output is automatically linked to the focusing distance, resulting in perfectly exposed macro shots.

With ratios of 1:1 or greater, any macro lens should be reversed, with the front element towards the camera. The correction of the lenses is set such that the distance of object to lens is greater than lens to camera. At a ratio of 1.01:1, however, this relationship reverses. For that reason, reversing ring BR-2A is offered for the N90/F90.

❒ **Bellows units -** The bellows unit is the most professional macro accessory, but it only allows stepless adjustment in the close-focus range, and can only be focused manually.

The original Nikon Bellows unit PB-6 is recommended, thanks to its stable and precise design. In order to simultaneously release the shutter and close the lens to the working aperture, you will need the magnetic double cable release AR-10. To attach it to the N90/F90, the MC-25 adapter is necessary.

The PG-2 focus rule is a useful instrument, allowing reproduction size (1:1 and greater) to be determined by the distance of the lens to the subject. Focus is then determined using the focus rule with the change in distance between the lens and subject.

It goes without saying that all Micro Nikkors can be used with the bellows unit.

❐ **Using enlarging lenses -** You can use good enlarging lenses like the EL Nikkors and Apo-Rodagons (from Rodenstock) for macro photography via adapter rings.

❐ **Slide duplication -** Duplicating slides falls within the realm of macro photography. Duplications guard against loss when sending slides to publications, agencies, to the ab, or to photo contests. For about $100 U.S., you can purchase a simple slide duplicator. In practical use, I found this relatively cheap Nikon accessory to be sharper than a non-Nikon that was ten times more expensive. The only disadvantage of the simple units is that the reproduction is slightly larger than 1:1, meaning that some of the original is cut off. If you want exact 1:1 or steplessly adjustable ratios, buy the PZ-6 duplication accessory for the PB-6, bellows unit. A macro lens is required as well.

Lastly, use special "slide duplicating film" from Kodak, which is processed E6. Duplications are too contrasty for normal slide films.

Lenses: Features and Quality

The quality of a lens can be viewed from many standpoints. You can look at its sharpness, distortion, light falloff, sharpness at close-up and at infinity, chromatic aberration, or mechanical durability and focusing speed.

Distortion and Falloff

This can be a problem in wide-angle lenses. Because of their construction, wide-angles show decidedly more light falloff than normal lenses when they are wide open. Super wide-angles suffer from distortion as well as falloff problems. These effects become more noticeable as the focal length shortens. Fortunately, however, such problems are for the most part corrected in modern quality lenses and should not be confused with typical wideangle perspective, which is actually a desired effect in some photographic situations.

Focal Optimization

In the past, lenses could not be optimized for both distance and closeups; they were optimized for either closeups or infinity. This means that while their faults were minimal at the close focus distance or at infinity, in-between was a different story. Additional moving elements have made it possible to correct close-up problems like pincushion distortion and various aperture problems. These lenses not only have two main element groups that move toward each other as in conventional lenses, but also a third group that moves in between them. Nikon's Close-Range Correction (CRC) makes it possible for the same lens to be used for both normal and close-up photography.

Chromatic Aberration and APO Lenses

Chromatic aberration has an undesirable effect at long focal lengths. Red, green, and blue light are not focused at the same plane, resulting in color fringing. All modern telephoto lenses are achromatic; corrected so that real rainbow effects are very seldom seen. Modern lenses achieve apochromatic correction through the use of low dispersion (LD) glass or extraordinary dispersion (ED) glass. These types of glass do not disperse light as much as ordinary types of optical glass, allowing lenses to be made with no dispersion evident in the final image.

Internal Focusing

When using the autofocusing capabilities of older telephoto lenses, the main element groups are moved with respect to each other, or all of the optical components are moved as a unit, resulting in a marked change in the overall length of the lens. The longer the focal length, the longer the extension, making telephoto lenses cumbersome and inexact as well as very slow. The solution is Nikon's line of internal focusing (IF) telephoto lenses. Focusing is accomplished by moving one component between the two main groups. The movement is extremely short and the overall length of the lens therefore remains completely constant. Such lenses are unbeatable in AF mode, and can be combined with a "floating element" automatic correction factor that results in even further improved image quality.

AF-I Nikkors

The unique feature of the AF-I Nikkors is that they have a built-in, super-fast focusing motor. It works in conjunction with the motor in the camera body for focusing speed never before available with Nikon equipment. Even the long telephoto lenses are lightning fast.

AF-I lenses can, of course, be focused manually with great precision. The best part is that the lens does not have to be switched from manual to autofocus mode. Simply turning the focusing ring temporarily overrides the autofocusing system.

Please note, however, that since the AF-I lenses' special options require a unique interaction with the camera, they are only fully compatible with the F4 and N90/F90. With other models, the AF-I Nikkors work in all exposure modes, but can only be focused manually.

AF-D Nikkors

The ROM chip in conventional AF Nikkors sends only information pertaining to the number of motor revolutions necessary to focus. The new AF-D Nikkors, on the other hand, send the actual focus distance. Because of this, use of the three-dimensional exposure and flash modes, incorporated into the N90/F90, is possible.

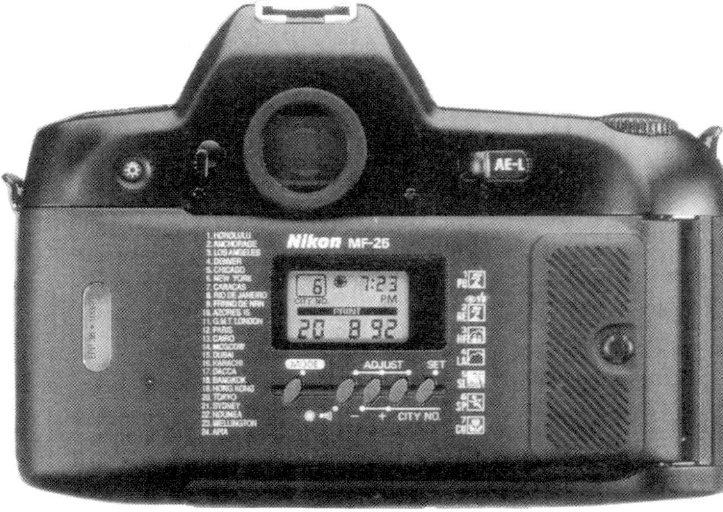

Data Back MF-25

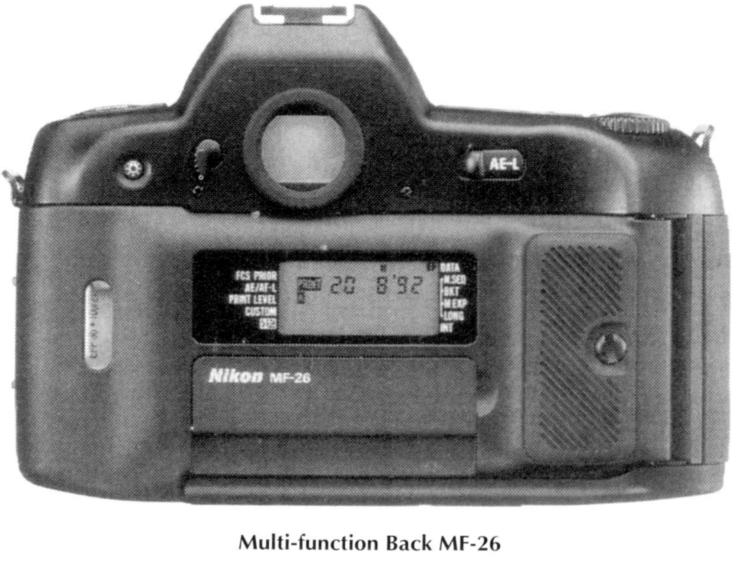

Multi-function Back MF-26

Programming the N90/F90

The N90/F90 comes out of the box programmed with 15 default functions. These functions can be adjusted when using the camera, but when the N90/F90 is reset, it reverts back to these defaults.

Reprogramming

Many of the N90/F90's functions can be reprogrammed by authorized Nikon service centers. The following is a list of reprogrammable functions:

1) Individual program curves by entering three distinct points on the curve.
2) Signal (warning) beeper's tone.
3) DX priority for film speed selection.
4) Optional simultaneous storage of AE and AF.
5) Automatic film rewind at the end of the roll.
6) Camera's time-out (between 4 and 60 seconds).
7) Continuous focusing during film transport in "S" mode.
8) Function of the AF-L button.
9) Long time exposures.
10) Exposure delay when using several cameras.
11) Data that is added to the frame.

Additionally, there are several functions available to the N90/F90 only when using the Multi-function Back MF-26.

Data Link System

Note: The following information is based only on vague information. I have not yet had the chance to test the Data Link in the field.

Available mid-1993, the Data Link enables the N90/F90 to be connected to the Sharp Wizard (8000) Electronic Organizers. These pocket computers are small databases in their non-photographic application (store addresses, telephone numbers, dates, notes, clock, calculator).

To convert the Wizard into a photographic tool, Nikon offers the connector cable MC-27 for the N90/F90 and a special "Chip card" that slides into the Electronic Organizer. When the Organizer is not connected (offline) several functions are available. It provides an instruction manual for the N90/F90, a photographic handbook with a glossary of terms and a collection of photographic equations, and a utility program to manage data gathered while working with the N90/F90.

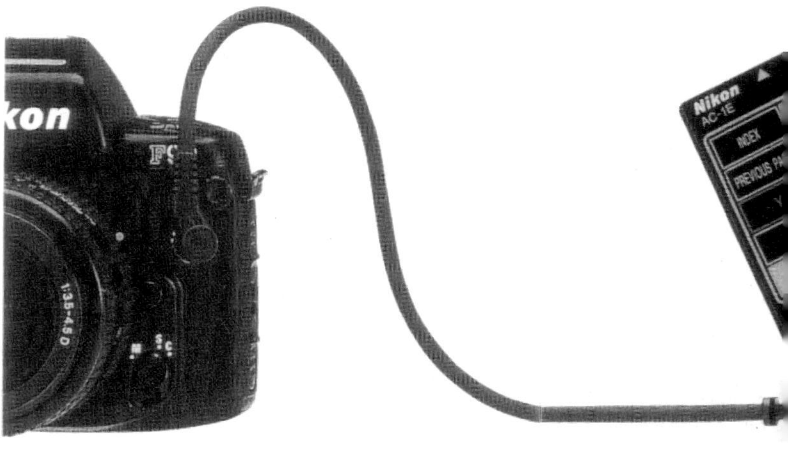

The Data Link System with IC card and electronic organizer.

When it is connected to the N90/F90, many camera fuctions are controllable with the computer. You can select the metering method, exposure mode (including Vari-programs), shutter speed setting, flash sync, self-timer functions, film transport mode, AF field size, film speed setting, exposure correction, AF focusing, and triggering.

The Verdict

With the Electronic Organizer, the N90/F90 becomes the world's first truly remote controlled camera. While many functions are just as easily controlled on the camera body itself, the setup is ideal in photographic reproduction or research applications.

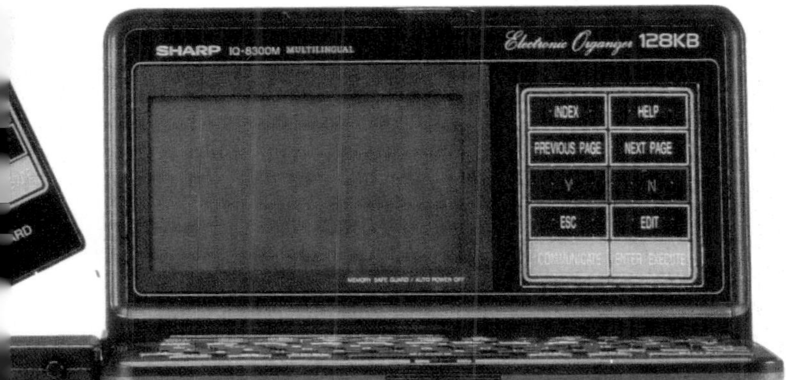

N90/F90 Accessories

It does not take long to figure out that dragging a jam-packed gadget bag through the countryside in order to take three pictures is overkill. On the other hand, though, the joy of photography quickly disappears if your camera outfit is badly lacking. The best rule of thumb is to be as complete as absolutely necessary and as scant as possible!

Vital Accessories

Like oil for your car, there are several accessories that you cannot live without.

❐ **UV or skylight filters -** You should always have a UV-blocking filter or a skylight filter in front of your lens. Even though this means that there are two more glass/air surfaces (resulting in higher risk of dispersion and refraction), the advantages far outweigh this small downside. Skylight and UV filters not only protect the lens' front element from finger prints and scratches, but also block damaging ultra-violet rays. The UV portion of sunlight reduces sharpness and causes inexplicable blue hazes, even with today's modern films. The UV filter only absorbs ultra-violet rays while the skylight filter also reduces the blue tones that are prevalent under cloudy skies, on the beach, in the mountains and at high noon. I have used a skylight filter in front of a myriad of lenses for many years since a blue cast on my slides bothers me a great deal more than the slightly warm color rendition the filter causes, but this is admittedly a matter of taste; purists often prefer a UV filter.

As protection for the front lens element, these filters are invaluable. A $30 filter is much less painful to replace than a $300 lens.

❐ **Lens hoods -** Sometimes called a sunshade, the hood can be more accurately described as a "stray light shade" and should always be used. This hoods prevent stray light from entering the lens, light that causes dispersion or even poor contrast or color saturation. If you shoot directly into the sun, however, not even a lens hood will help.

In the practical world of photography, lens hoods made of hard plastic or metal are preferable to those made of rubber. Flexible lens hoods often flip back if they are accidentally hit "in the heat of battle." Only in storage are they more practical.

❒ **Camera body cap** - An indispensable item, this cap should always be mounted on the camera when it is stored without a lens. As well as protecting it from dust, the cap prevents you from inadvertently touching the reflex mirror or the AF contacts when you remove the camera from the bag.

❒ **Rear lens cap** - Rear lens caps must be mounted onto the lens as soon as it is removed from the camera to prevent fingerprints, scratches, and damage to aperture or other mechanisms. Be careful though. These caps have been known to fall off at inopportune moment; never pull a lens out of your camera bag by grabbing onto the rear cap.

❒ **Front lens cap** - Unnecessary if you use a skylight or UV filter.

❒ **Camera bags** - Like most things in life, which camera bag to use is purely up to the photographer's taste. Metal cases that were so popular in earlier days are now generally only used for transport on airplanes or the like. Today's bags are compact outside and spacious within, and each manufacturer offers special features. Look for a bag that will help, and not hinder you. In terms of bulk, less is more. A bag that looks beautiful in the store may seem less appealing after you have lugged it around for a few weeks. And since cameras are almost always damaged outside the bag, heavy padding is superfluous and will only slow you down. Many professionals swear by bags made by Domke Photo Resources; they are functional down to the last stitch. But in the end, you must buy what fits your needs. Try several of them out, and don't skimp. A few extra dollars today will pay dividends tomorrow.

Lastly, be inconspicuous! A bag with NIKON written all over it is a prime target for thieves.

❒ **Electronic cable release** - Conventional cable releases cannot be connected to the N90/F90 without special adapters. If you need to expose without jarring the camera in repro work, microscopy, or long time exposures, the electronic cable release MC-20 is a good thing to have. The self-timer is not a viable alternative, as it does not enable a spontaneous exposure at a desired instant.

❒ **Assorted nic-nacs** - While they may seem insignificant, having things like a dust brush, lens tissue and cleaning fluid, a roll of black tape, spare batteries, a tripod quick-release plate, a film extractor, a gray card for precise light metering, a small note pad, and a permanent marker are easily carried and very functional. Someday you'll be happy to have these things with you.

Luxury Items

Some accessories may seem to be luxuries. Until you need them. Here are some that are not absolutely necessary, but are very nice to have.

❐ **Tripod -** A good tripod is often needed even with today's modern "electronic" cameras, especially when working with focal lengths over 300mm. Movement at the moment of exposure can result in blurred images.

❐ **Circular polarizers -** A polarizer reduces glare and reflection as well as cuts through mist in long distance shots. Depending on which way it is oriented on the lens, it will only allow light rays with certain polarity to pass through. By turning it, you can remove reflections from water, glass, and other shiny surfaces (except metal). In landscape shots, the light refracted through the mist has a different polarity than that coming directly from the subject. The mist can therefore be filtered out by the polarizer.

Since polarizers absorb a great deal of light, the exposure has to increase correspondingly. Polarizes are automatically accounted for in all of the N90/F90's exposure modes. Remember, though, that only circular polarizers will work. The AF sensor is confused by linear polarizers and automatic focusing can be affected.

❐ **Special-effect filters -** While a good shot may sometimes be made better by using creative filters, bad pictures cannot be made into creative masterpieces. I have tested over 90 of these filters and have generally been disappointed. Simply on the basis of physics and optics, these filters cannot produce the outstanding images shown in the manufacturer's brochure. Many of these adapters are dependent on the focal length, the distance between the filter and the lens's front element, the aperture, the focus distance, the highlight to shadow range, etc. To achieve the advertised results, you may even have to take several shots and then carefully put the slides on top of each other.

Keep in mind that there is always the possibility of interference with the autofocus sensor, and that you may have to switch to manual focus and exposure modes.

Care and Storage of Camera and Accessories

Your camera is an intricate instrument, but not as fragile as you may thing. Here are some things to keep in mind when caring for your camera.

Enough is Enough

A camera is not a toy for clean freaks in an attempt to keep your camera pristine, you may damage it. Be careful, use common sense, and don't get in over your head. If a repair requires precision screwdrivers and needle-nose pliers, take it to a professional.

Common Problems

There are several things that you must deal with in order to keep your camera running and taking good pictures.

❒ **Dust and sand** - These are two of a photographer's worst enemies. Any dust in the camera must be removed immediately or it could appear right in the middle of your next image. Soft dust brushes will generally take care of the problem.

Sand is fatal; if it gets into the shutter mechanism, your camera is as good as dead. When at the beach or in a desert sandstorm, always keep your equipment in an air-tight container.

❒ **Fingerprints** - If a fingerprint gets onto your lenses or filter, it should be removed immediately; the oil from your fingers can cause irreparable damage.

Lens fluid is available in all camera stores and should always be applied before using a static-eliminating cloth. Make sure that no sand particle or other hard object gets between the cloth and the lens. Work gently, and with circular strokes.

❒ **Do not oil** - Even the finest sewing machine oil should never be used on your camera or lenses. All oils harden after a while, binding moving parts rather than lubricating them. All cameras and lenses are lubricated for life at the factory, and even then, only in places that are inaccessible to you and me. If your camera is making strange noises or your lens' aperture ring is sticky, send the unit to Nikon or to the appropriate lens manufacturer.

❒ **Moisture** - A sturdy plastic pouch is an invaluable part of your camera's outfit. It protects from sand, rain, high humidity, and even from a dip in the pool. Remember, though, that such containers can cause condensation which is not only hazardous to the camera's electronics but also for the film in the camera. Pack your N90/F90 in plastic only when using a few packages of silica gel.

❐ **Condensation -** If you take your camera from a cold area to a warm one, it will instantly fog up. When this happens, carefully wipe the leans, and then leave it alone to dry. Only after the moisture is completely gone is it safe to pack it up and go home.

❐ **Leaking batteries -** If you do not intend to use your equipment for a long period of time, remove the batteries.

❐ **Recycle your flash -** If your flash sits idle for extended periods, put batteries in it from time to time and turn it on. After a few minutes, trigger it several times. Let it recycle, and then and turn it off without triggering it. This procedure keeps the capacitors in good working order. If you ignore your flash, it will eventually lose some or all of its power.

The Verdict

You have purchased a very expensive, state-of-the art piece of equipment. If it is working well, leave it alone. If it is not, have an authorized Nikon dealer look at it. Concentrate on taking beautiful pictures, and leave the screw-tightening to the experts.

A low camera angle produced this interesting juxtaposition of technology and nature. The satellite station antenna seems to be growing out of the grassy field. ⇨

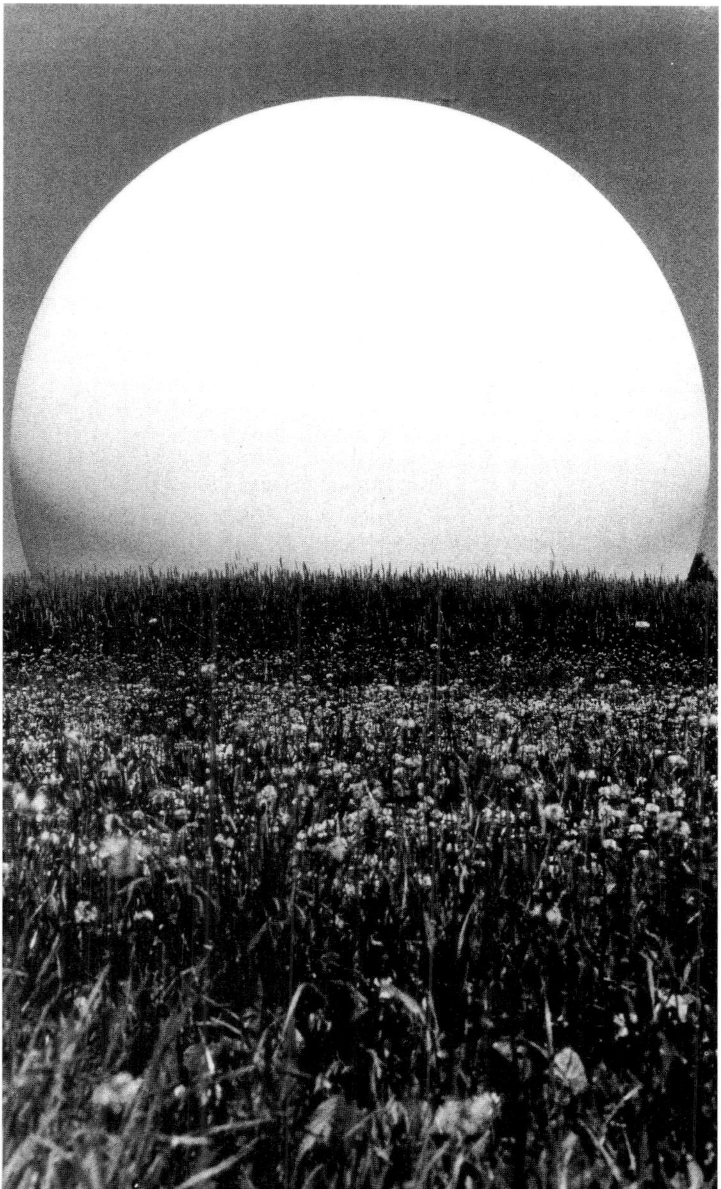

One Final Word

I hope that this manual has been informative and helpful for you. The N90/F90 is an extremely complex camera, and there is a danger that the pure pleasure of making pictures will be replaced with computer-controlled, scientifically-calculated processes. The N90/F90 is an amazing tool, but is useless without your imagination and skill, so have fun with it.

Happy Shooting!

N90/F90 Compatibility with Nikkor Lenses and Accessories

Lens/	Focusing System			Exposure Mode				Metering Method		
Accessory	Auto-focus	Manual with electronic assistance	Fully Manual	Program Mode	Shutter Priority	Aperture Priority	Manual	Matrix	Center-Weighted	Spot
All AF except for F3AF Nikkors	O	O	O	O	O	O	O	O*1	O	O
AI-P	O*2	O*3	O	O	O	O	O	O	O	O
AI and AI-S (including modified AI)	O*2	O*3	O	X	X	O	O	X	O	O
Medical-Nikkor 1:4/120mm IF	X	O	O	X	X	X	O*4	X	O*5	O*5
Reflex-Nikkor*6	X	X	O	X	X	O*7	O*7	X	O	O
PC-Nikkor*6	X	X	O	X	X	O*8	O*9	X	O	O
Teleconverter TC-16A	O*10	X	X	X	X	O	O	X	O	O
AI and AI-S Teleconverters (except TC-16A)	X	O*11	O	X	X	O	O	X	O	O
Bellows Unit PB-6	X	O*11	O	X	X	O*14	O*14	X	O	O
Extension Tubes "K"*12	X	O*11	O	X	X	O*15	O*15	X	O	O
Automatic Extension Tubes*13	X	O*11	O	X	X	O	O	X	O	O

O Compatible **X Incompatible**

*1 The camera automatically switches to 3D Matrix metering with type D Nikkors, and to 2D metering with others.
*2 The effective speed with the TC-16A must be at least f/5.6.
*3 With minimum speed of f/5.6.
*4 Use a shutter speed of 1/250 or longer.
*5 Since the aperture is connected to the focusing ring, the exposure setting is independent of the camera's metering system.
*6 Some lenses cannot be connected to the N90/F90.
*7 Fixed aperture.
*8 Set the selection ring and then store the exposure with the AE-L button before shifting.
*9 Set the selection ring and measure the exposure before shifting.
*10 With AI or AI-s Nikkors that have a maximum aperture of at least f/3.5. Some lenses can, however, be used with the TC-16A.
*11 The effective f-stop must be at least f/5.6.
*12 The K-1 ring cannot be mounted on AF Nikkors. Use the RK-11A or BR-6 instead.
*13 The PK-1, PK-2, PK-3, and PN-1 rings cannot be mounted on the N90/F90, and the PK-11 ring cannot be mounted on AF Nikkors.
*14 Exposure according to metered value with a stopped-down PB-6.
*15 Exposure metering according to working aperture.

The following Nikkors cannot be used with the N90/F90:

- Non-AI lenses
- 6mm f/5.6 fisheye
- 10mm f/5.6 OP-fisheye
- 200-600mm f/9.5 (serial numbers 280001-301922)
- 180-600mm f/8 ED (# 174041-174180)
- 360-1200mm f/11 ED (# 174031-174070)
- 400mm f/5.6 and 600mm f/5.6 with AU-1 installed
- PC 28mm f/4 (to # 180900)
- PC 35mm f/2.8 (# 851001-906200)*
- 1000mm f/11 mirror (# 142361-143000)*
- 2000mm f/11 mirror (# 200111-200310)*

* *Can be modified to work for a minimal cost. Consult your local Nikon dealer.*

Overview of AF Nikkor Lenses

Lens Description	Elements/ Groups	Angle of View(°)	Smallest Aperture	Close-focus Distance (m/ft.)	Macro (m)	Maximum Magnification Ratio	Filter Size (mm)	Lens Hood	Weight (g)	Size (mm)
16mm/2.8 D Fisheye	8-5	180	22	0.25/0.83	-	-	Bayonet	-	325	63.0x54.8
20mm/2.8 AF	12-9	94	22	0.25/0.83	-	1:8.4	62	HB-4	260	69.0x52.0
24mm/2.8 AF	9-9	84	22	0.30/1.0	-	1:8.8	52	HN-1	260	65.0x55.5
28mm/1.4 D AF	11-8	74	16	0.35/1.16	-	-	72	-	565	75.0x77.5
28mm/2.8 AF	5-5	74	22	0.30/1.0	-	1:7.6	52	HN-2	195	65.0x48.7
35mm/2.0 AF	6-5	62	22	0.25/0.83	-	1:4.2	52	HN-3	215	63.0x43.5
50mm/1.4 AF	7-6	46	16	0.45/1.5	-	1:6.8	52	HR-2	255	65.0x52.5
50mm/1.8 AF	6-5	46	22	0.45/1.5	-	1:6.6	52	HR-2	210	65.0x48.0
60mm/2.8 AF Micro	8-7	39°40′	32	0.22/0.73	-	1:1	62	HN-22	455	70.0x74.5
85mm/1.8 AF	6-6	28°30′	16	0.85/2.81	-	1:9.2	62	HN-23	415	71.0x69.0
105mm/2.0 D DC AF	6-6	23°20′	16	0.90/2.97	-	-	72	-	640	79.0x111
105mm/2.8 AF Micro	9-8	23°20′	32	0.31/1.02	-	1:1	52	HS-7	555	75.0x105
135mm/2.0 DC AF	7-6	18	16	1.1/3.63	-	1:70	72	BUILT-IN	870	79.0x128
180mm/2.8 IF-ED AF	8-6	13°40′	22	1.5/4.95	-	1:6.4	72	BUILT-IN	750	78.5x153
300mm/2.8 IF-ED AF	8-6	8°10′	22	3.0/9.90	-	1:8.4	39	BUILT-IN	2700	133.0x263
300mm/4.0 IF-ED AF	8-6	8°10′	32	2.5/8.25	-	1:70	39	BUILT-IN	1330	89.0x227
300mm/2.8 D IF-ED AF-I*	11-9	8°10′	22	2.5/8.25	-	-	39	HK-19	2950	124.0x241
400mm/2.8 D IF-ED AF-I*	10-7	6°10′	22	3.3/10.89	-	-	52	-	6300	158.0x375
600mm/4.0 D IF-ED AF-I*	9-7	4°10′	22	6.0/19.80	-	-	39	HK-18	6050	166.0x417
20-35mm/2.8 D AF	14-11	94-64	22	0.50/1.65	-	-	77	-	585	82.0x94.0
24-50mm/3.3-4.5 AS AF	9-9	84-46	22	0.60/1.98	0.5	1:8.0	62	HB-3	375	70.5x82.5

Lens Description	Elements/ Groups	Angle of View(°)	Smallest Aperture	Close-focus Distance (m/ft.)	Macro (m)	Maximum Magnification Ratio	Filter Size (mm)	Lens Hood	Weight (g)	Size (mm)
28-70mm/3.5- 4.5 AS AF	8-7	74-34°20′	22	0.50/1.65	0.39	1:4.6	52	HB-6	350	67.5x71.0
28-70mm/3.5- 4.5 D AF	8-7	74-34°20′	22	0.50/1.65	0.39	1:4.6	52	HB-6	355	67.5x71.0
28-85mm/3.3 AS AF	15-11	74-28°30′	22	0.80/2.64	0.23	1:3.4	62	HB-1	540	71.0x97.5
35-70mm/2.8 AF	15-12	62-34°20′	22	0.60/1.98	0.28	1:4.0	62	HB-1	665	72.0x105
35-70mm/2.8 D AF	15-12	62-34°20′	22	0.60/1.98	0.28	1:4.0	62	HB-1	675	71.5x105
35-70mm/3.3-4.5 AF	8-7	62-34°20′	22	0.50/1.65	0.35	1:4.4	52	HN-2	275	70.5x69.0
35-80mm/4.0-5.6 D	6-6	62-30°10′	22	0.50/1.65	0.35	?	52	?	255	66.5x60
35-105mm/3.5-4.5 AF	16-12	62-23°20′	22	1.4/4.42	0.28	1:4.0	52	HB-5	460	69.0x95.5
35-135mm/3.5-4.5 AF	15-12	62-18	22	1.5/4.95	0.40	1:4.0	52	HB-5	685	72.5x117
70-210mm/4.0-5.6 AF	12-9	34°20′-11°50′	32	1.5/4.95	1.2	1:4.5	62	HN-24	590	73.5x116
75-300mm/4.5-5.6 AF	13-11	31°10′-8°10′	32	3.0/9.90	1.5	1:3.8	62	HN-24	860	72.0x166
80-200mm/2.8 ED AF	16-11	30°10′-12°10′	22	1.8/5.94	1.5	1:5.9	77	HN-28	1200	85.5x184.5
80-200mm/2.8 ED AF	16-11	30°10′-12°10′	22	1.8/5.94	1.5	1:5.9	77	HB-7	1300	87.0x187
TC-16A AF**	5-5	-	-1.3 EV	****	-	-	-	-	150	69.0x30.0
TC-14E 1.4x I***	5-5	-	-1 EV	****	-	-	-	-	200	65x24,5
TC-20E ex I***	7-6		-2 EV	****	-	-	-	-	340	65x55

*** Autofocusing possible with N90/F90 and F4 only.**

**** Complete compatibility with N90/F90, F4, and N8008/F-801 only.**

***** Only in combination with AF-I-Nikkors**

****** Same as main lens without teleconverter.**

? Information not available as of publication date.

Notes